WeightWatchers

COOK SMART **simply suppers**

Easy, healthy recipes for fabulous evening meals

SIMON &
SCHUSTER

London • New York • Sydney • Toronto

First published in Great Britain by Simon & Schuster UK Ltd, 2009
A CBS Company

Weight Watchers Publications Team: Jane Griffiths, Donna Watts, Nina McKerlie and Fiona Smith

A selection of recipes and images appear courtesy of weightwatchers.co.uk. For more information about Weight Watchers Online, visit www.weightwatchers.co.uk

Photography by Steve Baxter, Iain Bagwell, Steve Lee and Juliet Piddington
Design and typesetting by James Marks
Printed and bound in China

A CIP catalogue for this book is available from the British Library

ISBN 978-1-84737-611-4

1 3 5 7 9 10 8 6 4 2

Pictured on the front cover: Lemon and Berry Creamy Pots page 150, Thai Chicken Soup page 10, Warm Spicy Sausage and Spinach Salad page 87, Spicy Vegetable Tagine page 132
Pictured on the back cover: Mediterranean Pasta Salad page 135, Parma Ham and Artichoke Pizza page 74, Chocolate Orange Treat page 140, Tarragon Chicken with Lemon Braised potatoes page 62
Pictured on the introduction: Thai Chicken Soup page 10, Cajun Pork Steaks with Sweet Potato Chips page 88, Caribbean Cod page 105, Lemon and Berry Creamy Pots page 150

POINTS ® value logo: You'll find this easy to read **POINTS** value logo on every recipe throughout this book. The logo represents the number of **POINTS** values per serving each recipe contains. For more information about Weight Watchers call 08457 123 000.

V This symbol denotes a vegetarian recipe and assumes that, where relevant, free range eggs, vegetarian cheese, vegetarian virtually fat free fromage frais and vegetarian low fat crème fraîche are used. Virtually fat free fromage frais and low fat crème fraîche may contain traces of gelatine so they are not always vegetarian. Please check the labels.

✱ This symbol denotes a dish that can be frozen.

Recipe notes
Egg size: Medium, unless otherwise stated.

All fruits and vegetables: Medium sized, unless otherwise stated.

Raw eggs: Only the freshest eggs should be used. Pregnant women, the elderly and children should avoid recipes with eggs that are not fully cooked or raw.

Stock: Stock cubes used in recipes, unless otherwise stated. These should be prepared according to packet instructions.

Recipe timings: These are approximate and meant to be guidelines. Please note that the preparation time includes all the steps up to and following the main cooking time(s).

Low fat polyunsaturated margarine: Use brands such as Flora Light, St Ivel Gold and Benecol Light.

Contents

Introduction

So many of us rush our evening meal or depend on fast food and takeaways. Time is often short, and the last thing many people want to do at the end of a busy day is to start cooking.

This book is designed to help. It is full of ideas for delicious, healthy and filling meals suitable for family and friends. Many are quick or easy to make, and many are suitable for freezing, meaning it is simple to prepare meals for the week ahead and defrost them as they are needed

There are ideas for special occasions in here too, and starters and desserts for those times when a simple main course just won't do.

About Weight Watchers

For more than 40 years Weight Watchers has been helping people around the world to lose weight using a long term sustainable approach. Weight Watchers successful weight loss system is based on four tried and trusted principles:

- Eating healthily
- Being more active
- Adjusting behaviour to help weight loss
- Getting support in weekly meetings

Our unique **POINTS** system empowers you to manage your food plan and make wise recipe choices for a healthier, happier you.

Basic Ingredients

Milk

Always use skimmed milk, rather than whole or semi-skimmed, unless otherwise stated in the recipe.

Eggs

Use medium sized eggs, unless otherwise stated in the recipe. Always bring eggs to room temperature before using. A cold egg won't whisk well and the shell will crack if placed in hot water.

Fats and oils

The majority of recipes use low fat cooking spray rather than oil. Low fat cooking spray can be either olive oil or sunflower oil based. Try both and see which you prefer.

Generally, low fat polyunsaturated margarine is used in recipes rather than butter.

Cheese and yogurt

The cheese used in these recipes is low fat Cheddar, low fat soft cheese or virtually fat free fromage frais. Many recipes use yogurt. Always choose either 0% fat Greek yogurt or low fat natural or fruit yogurt. Quark – a very low fat soft cheese made with skimmed milk – is also used. All of these products are easy to find in a supermarket.

Fruit and vegetables

Make sure your family eats plenty of fruit and vegetables, preferably at least five portions a day. Try putting a fruit snack in lunchboxes and always offer your family at least one vegetable with the main meal. Filling up on fruit and vegetables will also stop you from feeling hungry, so you are less likely to snack on fatty and sugary foods.

There are plenty of vegetarian recipes in the book, including healthy salads and soups, as well as suggestions for vegetable accompaniments.

Planning Ahead

When you're going around the supermarket it is tempting to pick up foods you like and put them in your trolley without thinking about how you will use them. So, a good plan is to decide what dishes you want to cook before you go shopping, check your store cupboard ingredients and make a list of what you need. You'll save time by not drifting aimlessly around the supermarket picking up what you fancy. You might even have time for a cup of tea or coffee.

Store Cupboard Suggestions

artichokes, canned

artificial sweetener

bay leaves

borlotti beans, canned

cannellini beans, canned

capers

chick peas, canned

chilli (flakes, powder)

chocolate (70%+)

cloves

cornflour

couscous

flour (plain, brown, wholemeal, self raising)

fish sauce, Thai

fruit, canned in natural juice

fruit, dried (raisins, sultanas, apricots, blueberries, etc.)

garlic cloves

gelatine

gravy granules

herbs, dried (mixed, oregano, thyme, etc.)

honey, runny

jam, reduced sugar

kidney beans, canned

lemons

lentils (red and brown)

low fat coconut milk

low fat cooking spray

mayonnaise, extra light

mushrooms, dried

mustard (English and wholegrain)

noodles (rice and egg)

nuts

oil (olive and sunflower)

olives in brine (black)

passata

pasta

pastry, filo

peas (frozen)

peppercorns

pine nut kernels

pizza bases

polenta (cornmeal)

rice (basmati, brown and risotto)

salt (sea salt or low sodium)

seeds (caraway, fennel, pumpkin and sesame)

spices, ground (coriander, cumin, cinnamon, nutmeg, ginger, Chinese 5 spice, allspice, paprika, cayenne pepper, curry powder)

soy sauce, light

stock cubes (vegetable, chicken and beef)

sugar (caster, demerara, muscovado)

sweet chilli sauce

sweetcorn, canned or frozen

Thai curry paste

tomato ketchup

tomato purée

tomatoes, canned

tuna, canned in brine or spring water

vanilla essence

vinegar (balsamic, rice, red wine, white wine)

Soups and Starters

No matter what time of year, soup is always welcome. Try filling favourites such as Spiced Tomato and Lentil Soup or Mediterranean Fish Soup. If it's a starter for a meal you're looking for, how about Italian Garlic Toasts or Spicy Prawn Cakes? They're all delicious and easy to make.

Make a simple supper a bit more special with a delicious soup or starter

Thai Chicken Soup

With the fragrant flavours of Thailand and the creaminess of coconut milk, this soup is hard to resist.

Serves 4

low fat cooking spray
1 stick of lemongrass, chopped
1 cm (½ inch) fresh root ginger, peeled and
    chopped finely
2 garlic cloves, crushed
2 x 165 g (5¾ oz) skinless, boneless chicken
    breasts, sliced into strips
1 small butternut squash, peeled, de-seeded
    and diced
1 teaspoon Thai curry paste
850 ml (1½ pints) chicken stock
100 ml (3½ fl oz) low fat coconut milk
125 g (4 oz) baby spinach
3 spring onions, sliced finely
3 tablespoons flaked almonds, toasted
salt and freshly ground black pepper

3½ *POINTS* values per serving
13½ *POINTS* values per recipe

C   **200 calories** per serving

Takes **20 minutes** to prepare, **20 minutes** to cook

✱   not recommended

1   Spray a non stick frying pan with the cooking spray and heat until hot. Stir fry the lemongrass, ginger and garlic for 2–3 minutes, adding a splash of water if they start to stick.

2   Spray the chicken with the cooking spray and add the chicken to the pan. Stir fry for 5–6 minutes before adding the butternut squash and Thai curry paste. Stir well to coat the chicken and vegetables with the flavourings.

3   Pour in the chicken stock and bring to a simmer. Cook for 15 minutes.

4   Add the coconut milk, spinach and spring onions. Simmer for a further 4–5 minutes to heat everything through and wilt the spinach.

5   Season to taste and serve sprinkled with toasted, flaked almonds.

Tip The outer leaves of lemongrass can be very tough, always remove a few layers before chopping or slicing the inside.

Variation This soup could be made with 175 g (6 oz) prawns instead of the chicken – add them in step 2 with the butternut squash, for 3 *POINTS* values per serving.

Hungarian Goulash Soup

Minced pork or turkey will be equally as delicious as the traditional beef in this spicy, rich soup. It is particularly good garnished with a swirl of low fat natural yogurt.

Serves 4

175 g (6 oz) extra lean beef mince
2 onions, chopped finely
1 celery stick, chopped
1 red, green or yellow pepper, de-seeded
  and chopped
2 teaspoons paprika
1 teaspoon ground cumin
690 g (1 lb 8 oz) chunky passata
600 ml (20 fl oz) vegetable stock
1 teaspoon sugar
40 g (1½ oz) small pasta shapes
1 tablespoon fresh parsley, chopped
salt and freshly ground black pepper
20 g (¾ oz) very low fat natural yogurt, to serve

1 Dry fry the minced beef in a large, lidded, non stick pan until browned. Add the onions, celery and pepper and sauté for 5 minutes, stirring frequently.

2 Reduce the heat, stir in the paprika and cumin and cook for a minute. Add the passata, stock, sugar and pasta. Cover and leave to simmer for 25 minutes, stirring occasionally.

3 Stir in the chopped parsley and season to taste. Serve, piping hot, ladled into warm soup bowls with a spoonful of yogurt on top.

1½ **POINTS** values per serving
6½ **POINTS** values per recipe

C 178 **calories** per serving

Takes **10 minutes** to prepare,
25 minutes to cook

* not recommended

Chestnut Soup with Croûtons

A rich and warming soup to serve as a seasonal supper party starter or as a warming lunch.

Serves 4

1 litre (1¾ pints) vegetable stock
1 leek, sliced
2 carrots, sliced
1 celery stick, sliced
435 g (15½ oz) can chestnut purée,
   unsweetened
2 medium slices brown bread, crusts removed
low fat cooking spray
2 teaspoons dried sage, or 16 fresh sage leaves
½ tablespoon caraway seeds
4 chestnuts, peeled and roughly chopped

1 Add the stock to a large, lidded pan and bring to the boil. Add the vegetables, cover and simmer for 20 minutes until all the vegetables are tender.

2 Add the chestnut purée. Transfer to a blender, or use a hand blender, and blend until smooth. Return to the pan, bring back to the boil and keep simmering over a low heat until ready to serve.

3 Cut each slice of bread into 16 squares. Spray a small, non stick frying pan with the cooking spray and heat until hot. Add the bread and cook over a medium heat for 2 minutes. Turn the squares over and cook for another minute until golden. Add the sage, caraway seeds and chopped chestnuts and cook, stirring for 1–2 minutes or until the sage leaves begin to toast and the nuts turn golden.

4 Serve the soup in warm bowls topped with the croûtons, sage, seeds and chestnuts.

4½ *POINTS* values per serving
18½ *POINTS* values per recipe

C   221 calories per serving

Takes 10 minutes to prepare,
20 minutes to cook

V

✻   not recommended

Mediterranean Fish Soup

If you're looking for a comforting meal, this hearty soup is packed with flavour; it's a complete meal in a bowl.

Serves 6

1 red and 1 yellow pepper, quartered and
  de-seeded
low fat cooking spray
1 large onion, sliced thinly
½ fennel bulb, sliced thinly
100 ml (3½ fl oz) white wine
3 garlic cloves, sliced finely
zest and juice of 1 small orange
a pinch of saffron threads
850 ml (1½ pints) fish stock
230 g can chopped tomatoes
200 g (7 oz) baby new potatoes, quartered
250 g (9 oz) skinless, boneless white fish
  fillet (e.g. monkfish or coley), chopped
  roughly
250 g (9 oz) frozen mixed seafood, defrosted
1 tablespoon chopped fresh parsley
freshly ground black pepper

1½ **POINTS** values per serving
9½ **POINTS** values per recipe

C 141 calories per serving

Takes **20 minutes** to prepare,
30 minutes to cook

✱ not recommended

1 Preheat the grill and place the peppers on the grill rack, skin side up. Grill for 6–8 minutes or until the skin is blistered. Transfer to a bowl, cover and leave to cool for 10 minutes or so, then peel off and discard the skin and roughly chop the peppers.

2 Meanwhile, spray a large, lidded saucepan with the cooking spray. Stir in the onion and fennel and cook gently for 10 minutes until softened, but not coloured. Add a splash of water if they start to stick.

3 Increase the heat, pour in the wine and stir in the garlic. Cook for about 2 minutes or until the wine has evaporated.

4 Add the orange zest and juice, saffron, fish stock, tomatoes and potatoes. Season with black pepper to taste and bring to a simmer. Cover and cook for 20 minutes.

5 Stir the peppers and any pepper juices that collected in the bowl into the pan, along with the chopped fish. Replace the lid and gently poach for 3 minutes.

6 Finally, stir in the mixed seafood and heat through for 2 minutes. Serve ladled into warmed bowls and scatter the parsley on top.

Variation For a Mediterranean vegetable soup, use vegetable stock instead of fish stock, omit the fish fillet and mixed seafood, and add two diced courgettes along with the grilled peppers. This will reduce the **POINTS** value to ½ per serving.

Courgette and Coriander Soup

A lovely fresh-flavoured and bright green summery soup.

Serves 2

low fat cooking spray
½ teaspoon ground coriander seeds
1 garlic clove, crushed
1 large onion, sliced thinly
**500 g (1 lb 2 oz) courgettes, peeled and
   chopped roughly**
600 ml (1 pint) vegetable stock
**a bunch of fresh coriander, including roots
   if possible, washed and chopped**
salt and freshly ground black pepper

1 Spray a large, non stick saucepan with the cooking spray and stir fry the coriander seeds, garlic and onion for 5 minutes, until softened, adding a little water if they start to stick.

2 Add the courgettes, stock, seasoning and the chopped stems and roots of the coriander. Bring to the boil and then simmer for 5 minutes, until the courgettes are tender. Add the coriander leaves, but reserve a little for garnishing.

3 In a food processor, or using a hand blender, liquidise the soup. Return to the pan, warm through, check the seasoning and then serve garnished with the reserved coriander leaves.

0 POINTS values per serving
0 POINTS values per recipe

C   **90 calories** per serving

Takes **15 minutes** to prepare,
15 minutes to cook

V

✱   recommended

Spiced Tomato and Lentil Soup

With plenty of fibre and protein from the lentils, this filling soup is a great standby to keep in the fridge for when you are short of time.

Serves 6

1 onion, chopped finely
2 carrots, peeled and diced
150 g (5½ oz) red lentils, rinsed
2 x 400 g cans chopped tomatoes
1 tablespoon ground cumin
1 teaspoon medium curry powder
1.2 litres (2 pints) vegetable stock
3 tablespoons chopped fresh coriander
freshly ground black pepper

1 Place all the ingredients except for the coriander and black pepper in a large lidded saucepan. Bring to a simmer, cover and cook for 30 minutes or until the lentils are completely soft.

2 Let the soup cool slightly, then liquidise in batches in a food processor or use a hand blender. Season with black pepper to taste and serve with the coriander scattered on top.

1 *POINTS* value per serving
7 *POINTS* values per recipe

c 123 calories per serving

Takes 10 minutes to prepare, 30 minutes to cook

v

* recommended

Serving suggestion This soup tastes fantastic with a spoonful of low fat natural yogurt, for an additional ½ *POINTS* value per serving.

Prawn Noodle Soup

This Oriental soup has a deliciously delicate and tasty flavour.

Serves 4

90 g (3¼ oz) egg noodles, broken roughly
low fat cooking spray
2 garlic cloves, crushed
1 cm (½ inch) fresh root ginger, peeled and
    chopped finely
4 spring onions, sliced finely
240 g (8½ oz) fresh, raw king prawns
1.2 litres (2 pints) hot vegetable stock
1 small leek, sliced thinly
salt and freshly ground black pepper

2 POINTS values per serving
7 POINTS values per recipe

C   **123 calories** per serving

Takes **25 minutes**

*   not recommended

1 Bring a medium saucepan of water to the boil and add the noodles. Simmer for 4 minutes. Drain and set aside.

2 Spray a medium saucepan with low fat cooking spray. Add the garlic, ginger and spring onions and stir fry for 2–3 minutes, adding a little water if they start to stick.

3 Add the prawns and stir fry for a further 1–2 minutes before adding the stock. Simmer for 2 minutes.

4 Add the noodles and leek to the pan and cook for a further 2–3 minutes.

5 Check the seasoning and serve in warmed bowls.

Variation You can use 240 g (8½ oz) lean pork strips instead of prawns – just stir fry the pork for slightly longer in step 3 before adding the stock, for 2½ **POINTS** values per serving.

Goat's Cheese and Chive Dip with Cucumber Sticks

2 POINTS VALUE

Soft goat's cheese has a very mild flavour, so don't be scared to give it a go in this creamy dip.

Serves 8

300 g (10½ oz) soft goat's cheese
150 g (5½ oz) low fat natural yogurt
1 garlic clove, crushed
2 heaped tablespoons snipped chives
2 large cucumbers, cut into batons
freshly ground black pepper

1 Simply mix the goat's cheese with the yogurt, garlic, chives and black pepper and spoon into a small serving bowl.

2 Surround with the cucumber sticks for dipping.

2 **POINTS** values per serving
17½ **POINTS** values per recipe

C 211 **calories** per serving

Takes **5 minutes**

V

✳ not recommended

Italian Garlic Toasts (Bruschetta)

This very simple recipe can be used as a base for savoury toppings like cheese and tomato or ham and mustard.

Serves 4

4 thick slices of bread, from a bloomer or rustic loaf
1 garlic clove
4 large plum tomatoes, diced
4 teaspoons extra virgin olive oil
basil leaves, to garnish
sea salt and freshly ground black pepper

1 Preheat the grill to medium hot. Toast the bread until golden on both sides. Cut the garlic clove in half and rub the cut side over the toast.

2 Spread the tomatoes over the toast. Dribble over the olive oil and scatter over the sea salt and black pepper. Serve while still hot, garnished with the basil leaves.

2½ **POINTS** values per serving
9½ **POINTS** values per recipe

C 140 **calories** per serving

Takes **5 minutes**

V

∗ not recommended

Smoked Mackerel Pâté

A robustly flavoured, creamy textured fresh pâté that is delicious served with two crispbreads per person, for a **POINTS** value of 1 per serving.

Serves 6

275 g (9½ oz) smoked mackerel fillets
2 tablespoons horseradish sauce
2 tablespoons virtually fat free fromage frais
freshly ground black pepper
6 wedges of lemon, to serve

3½ **POINTS** values per serving
20 **POINTS** values per recipe

c **145 calories** per serving

Takes **20 minutes**

* recommended

1 Remove the skin from the mackerel fillets and flake the fish into a bowl, removing any bones that you find.

2 Add the horseradish, fromage frais and black pepper and stir together. Pack into ramekins and serve with lemon wedges.

Tip This pâté keeps in the fridge for up to three days.

Cannellini Bean Pâté

Delicious served with two water biscuits and chunky sticks of cucumber and celery, for an additional 1 *POINTS* value.

Serves 4

410 g can cannellini beans, rinsed
  and drained
150 g (5½ oz) low fat soft cheese
1 garlic clove, crushed
3 tablespoons low fat mayonnaise
salt and freshly ground black pepper

3 *POINTS* values per serving
12 *POINTS* values per recipe

C 135 calories per serving

Takes 10 minutes + 2 hours chilling

V

✳ recommended

1 Place the cannellini beans in a food processor with the low fat soft cheese, garlic, mayonnaise and seasoning. Blend until smooth.

2 Transfer the pâté to a bowl, cover and chill for 2 hours before serving.

Variation Canned beans make the perfect base for vegetarian pâtés. Try using butter beans instead of cannellini beans. The *POINTS* values per serving will remain the same.

Marinated Mushroom Antipasto

This flavoursome dish can be served as a starter, accompaniment to a main dish or as a light lunch.

Serves 2

low fat cooking spray
1 garlic clove, crushed
450 g (1 lb) mushrooms, sliced
a few sprigs of fresh rosemary, chopped
zest and juice of ½ a lemon
1 tablespoon virtually fat free fromage frais
salt and freshly ground black pepper

1 Spray a non stick frying pan with the cooking spray. Stir fry the garlic for a few moments, until golden, then add the mushrooms, rosemary and seasoning.

2 Stir fry on a high heat until the mushrooms release their juices and then become dry again. Squeeze over the lemon juice and scatter with the zest then remove from the heat, allow to cool slightly, and stir in the fromage frais.

0 *POINTS* values per serving
½ *POINTS* value per recipe

C **40 calories** per serving

Takes **10 minutes**

V

* not recommended

Spicy Prawn Cakes

Great for a dinner party starter or nibble, these yummy prawn cakes can be made ahead and simply reheated just before your guests arrive.

Serves 4

For the prawn cakes

200 g (7 oz) frozen raw peeled tiger prawns, defrosted
200 g (7 oz) skinless, boneless white fish fillets (e.g. monkfish or coley), chopped roughly
1 tablespoon red Thai curry paste

1 tablespoon cornflour
4 spring onions, sliced finely
low fat cooking spray

For the dipping sauce

juice of a lime
4 tablespoons sweet chilli sauce
1 heaped tablespoon chopped fresh coriander

1 Place the prawns, fish, curry paste and cornflour in a food processor and blend until finely chopped. Remove the mixture from the food processor and place in a bowl. Mix in the spring onions, cover and chill in the fridge for 30 minutes. To make the dipping sauce, mix all the ingredients together in a small bowl and set aside.

2 Using your hands, carefully shape the mixture into 12 small cakes. Spray a large, non stick frying pan with the cooking spray and place on a medium to high heat. Add six prawn cakes and fry for 2 minutes on each side until browned and firm. Keep warm while you cook the remaining prawn cakes. Serve with the dipping sauce.

2 **POINTS** values per serving
7½ **POINTS** values per recipe

C 136 calories per serving

Takes **20 minutes + 30 minutes** chilling

* not recommended

Tip To reheat, spread out in a single layer on a baking tray, cover with foil and heat through for 10 minutes in an oven preheated to Gas Mark 4/180°C/fan oven 160°C.

Baked Tomatoes with Sweetcorn and Mozzarella

Based on the popular summer salad; here is a hot version for a warming starter.

Serves 4

4 large plum tomatoes
198 g can sweetcorn, drained
4 large fresh basil leaves, torn
125 g (4½ oz) mozzarella light cheese,
    drained and sliced into eight
salt and freshly ground black pepper
4 medium crusty bread rolls, to serve

4½ POINTS values per serving
19 POINTS values per recipe

C **123 calories** per serving

Takes **10 minutes** to prepare, **15 minutes** to cook

V

✽ not recommended

1 Preheat the oven to Gas Mark 6/200°C/fan oven 180°C. Halve the tomatoes lengthways. Scoop out and discard the core and seeds. Place the tomatoes in a shallow roasting tin and lightly season.

2 Spoon the sweetcorn into the tomato shells and top with the basil and a slice of mozzarella.

3 Bake for 15 minutes, until the tomatoes have softened. Remove from the oven and place under a hot grill for a minute or two, just to brown the cheese. Serve at once, accompanied by the crusty rolls.

Accompaniments

If you struggle to get your family to eat vegetables, try some of these dressed-up versions such as Braised Red Cabbage, Cauliflower Cheese, or Ratatouille. Tomato and Basil Dressing will help even the most fastidious eater enjoy salads or vegetables.

Turn plain vegetables into delicious accompaniments

French Style Braised Peas and Carrots

A tasty, country style French dish that makes the perfect accompaniment to grilled or roast meat or fish.

Serves 4

low fat cooking spray
a small bunch of spring onions, sliced finely
200 g (7 oz) baby carrots, washed,
    and larger ones sliced
200 ml (7 fl oz) vegetable stock
200 g (7 oz) frozen petit pois
1 Romaine lettuce, shredded
salt and freshly ground black pepper

½ *POINTS* value per serving
2½ *POINTS* values per recipe

C **50 calories** per serving

Takes **20 minutes**

V

✱ not recommended

1 Spray a large, lidded saucepan with the cooking spray and fry the spring onions for a few minutes, until softened, adding a little water if they start to stick. Add the carrots and stock and stir.

2 Bring to the boil and then simmer for 5 minutes before adding the petit pois and the lettuce. Cover the pan. Return to the boil for a further 4 minutes. Season and serve.

Green Beans with Rosemary

A great example of the Italian cucina povera – the use of inexpensive ingredients in the simplest ways – with delicious results.

Serves 4

500 g (1 lb 2 oz) green beans, topped
1 teaspoon olive, walnut or hazelnut oil
a few sprigs of fresh rosemary, chopped, plus a
few whole sprigs for garnishing
2 garlic cloves, sliced finely
1½ teaspoons red or white wine vinegar
salt and freshly ground black pepper

1 Bring a saucepan of water to the boil and blanch the beans for 4–5 minutes, until they are al dente and still bright green. Drain them and run under cold water to refresh.

2 Toss the beans with the other ingredients, season and serve garnished with a few sprigs of rosemary.

0 POINTS values per serving
1 POINTS value per recipe

C   **45 calories** per serving

Takes **10 minutes**

V   **Vg**

✱   not recommended

Braised Red Cabbage

This slightly sweet and sour cabbage is cooked until it is meltingly soft and delicious.

Serves 4

1 red cabbage, quartered and shredded finely
1 tablespoon white wine vinegar
2 dessert apples, peeled, cored and grated
salt and freshly ground black pepper

1 Put all the ingredients in a large, lidded saucepan with 100 ml (3½ fl oz) water. Cover and bring to the boil, then simmer on a low heat for 45 minutes or until the cabbage is meltingly soft and the liquid has almost gone. Season and serve.

½ *POINTS* value per serving
1½ *POINTS* values per recipe

C **35 calories** per serving

Takes **5 minutes** to prepare,
45 minutes to cook

V **Vg**

* not recommended

Tip This dish keeps well in the fridge for up to three days, and actually improves in flavour.

Ratatouille

This is a great way to use up vegetables and can be left to cook while you get on with the main dish.

Serves 4

low fat cooking spray
1 large onion, sliced
2 garlic cloves, chopped
1 large aubergine, sliced
2 courgettes, sliced
1 green pepper, de-seeded and sliced
200 g can chopped tomatoes
a bunch of basil
salt and freshly ground black pepper

0 POINTS values per serving
0 POINTS values per recipe

C **55 calories** per serving

Takes **15 minutes** to prepare,
60 minutes to cook

V

✱ not recommended

1 Spray a large, lidded pan with the cooking spray, then fry the onion, with a couple of tablespoons of water if it starts to stick, for 4 minutes. Add the garlic and cook for 1 minute.

2 Add the aubergine, courgettes, green pepper and seasoning. Cover and simmer for 40 minutes.

3 Add the tomatoes and basil and simmer, uncovered, for 20 minutes.

Lemon and Mint Chick Peas

Chick peas are fantastic at soaking up flavours and make a delicious and nutritious alternative to rice or pasta.

Serves 4

low fat cooking spray
½ teaspoon cumin seeds
1 large onion, chopped finely
2 garlic cloves, crushed
2.5 cm (1 inch) fresh root ginger, peeled and chopped finely
400 g can chick peas, drained and rinsed
zest and juice of ½ a lemon
100 ml (3½ fl oz) vegetable stock
a large bunch of mint, chopped
a pinch of freshly grated nutmeg
2 tablespoons virtually fat free fromage frais
salt and freshly ground black pepper

1 Heat a large, lidded saucepan, spray with the cooking spray and fry the cumin seeds until they pop. Add the onion, garlic and ginger and a few tablespoons of water. Stir fry for a few minutes or until the onion is soft.

2 Add the chick peas, lemon zest and juice, stock, mint, nutmeg and seasoning and stir together. Cook, covered, for 5 minutes. Remove from the heat and then stir in the fromage frais. Serve hot or cold.

2 *POINTS* values per serving
8½ *POINTS* values per recipe

C **100 calories** per serving

Takes **15 minutes**

V

✳ not recommended

Tomato and Basil Dressing

This fresh dressing is good on pasta salads or drizzled over steamed vegetables as well as on leafy salads. Use ripe tomatoes for a fully rounded flavour.

Serves 2

2 ripe tomatoes
½ small garlic clove, crushed (optional)
6 large basil leaves, shredded
½ teaspoon red or white wine vinegar
½ teaspoon tomato purée
salt and freshly ground black pepper

1 Cut a cross in the base of each tomato, place in a bowl and cover with boiling water. Leave to stand for 1 minute, or until the skins loosen.

2 Drain, then peel off the skins and roughly chop the flesh and seeds.

3 Place in a blender with the remaining ingredients, season and whizz to a smooth purée. Add a little cold water to thin the dressing down if you wish. If you don't have a blender or food processor, chop the tomatoes finely and mash all the ingredients together with a fork.

0 POINTS values per serving
0 POINTS values per recipe

16 calories per serving

Takes **5 minutes**

V **Vg**

✱ not recommended

Sicilian Aubergines (Caponata)

Here is a delicious low fat dish that creates something wonderful from aubergines.

Serves 4

2 tablespoons pine kernels
low fat cooking spray
1 onion, sliced finely
500 g (1 lb 2 oz) aubergines, diced small
1 teaspoon dried oregano or 1 tablespoon
    chopped fresh oregano
400 g can chopped tomatoes
1 tablespoon honey
50 g (1¾ oz) green or black olives, stoned
    and chopped roughly
3 tablespoons capers, rinsed
1 tablespoon red wine vinegar
salt and freshly ground black pepper

1½ **POINTS** values per serving
5½ **POINTS** values per recipe

C   150 **calories** per serving

Takes **20 minutes** to prepare, **35 minutes**
to cook + cooling time

V

✱   not recommended

1 Toast the pine kernels in a dry frying pan until golden brown. Spray a large, lidded frying pan with the cooking spray and fry the onion for about 4 minutes until soft. Add the aubergines and oregano and cook, turning frequently, for 5 minutes.

2 Add all the remaining ingredients, except the pine kernels. Cover and simmer for 35 minutes.

3 Taste and adjust the seasoning, adding more vinegar or honey if necessary to achieve a good sweet-and-sour balance.

4 For the best flavour, allow the caponata to cool to room temperature and then scatter over the pine kernels just before serving.

Tip Caponata tastes even better if it is left overnight in the fridge and then brought back to room temperature again before serving.

Celeriac Mash with Onion Gravy

Good served with low fat sausages, grilled fish or meat.

Serves 4

low fat cooking spray
4 red or white onions, sliced
a small bunch of thyme, tough stems removed,
**   tender stems and leaves chopped**
1 celeriac (about 600 g/1 lb 5 oz), peeled and
**   cut into small even sized chunks**
500 g (1 lb 2 oz) floury potatoes, such as Red
**   Rooster or Maris Piper, cut into even sized**
**   chunks**
100 g (3½ oz) virtually fat free fromage frais
300 ml (10 fl oz) vegetable stock
salt and freshly ground black pepper

1 Heat a large, lidded saucepan and spray with the cooking spray. Add the onions and stir fry for a few minutes. Season, add the thyme and a few tablespoons of water.

2 Cover the pan with a sheet of baking parchment and a lid and cook on the lowest heat for 20–30 minutes, until the onions are soft and caramelised, stirring very occasionally and scraping any stuck on bits back in.

3 Meanwhile, put the celeriac and potatoes in a large saucepan of cold water and bring to the boil. Reduce the heat and simmer for 20 minutes, until the vegetables are tender.

4 Drain the celeriac and potatoes and return to the pan. Season and mash until smooth. Stir in the fromage frais and keep warm.

5 Remove the lid and paper from the onions, turn up the heat and add the stock. Bring to the boil and allow to boil rapidly, stirring and scraping the bottom of the pan, until the gravy is reduced and thickened. Check the seasoning and serve with the mash.

1½ **POINTS** values per serving
6 **POINTS** values per recipe

c 175 **calories** per serving

Takes **15 minutes** to prepare,
30 minutes to cook

v

✱ recommended

Tip Cut the potatoes and celeriac into the same size pieces to ensure even cooking.

Cauliflower Cheese

Serves 4

450 g (1 lb) cauliflower, broken
   into florets
600 ml (1 pint) skimmed milk
50 g (1¾ oz) plain flour
25 g (1 oz) low fat polyunsaturated
   margarine
75 g (2¾ oz) extra mature Cheddar
   cheese

2 teaspoons wholegrain mustard
1 tablespoon finely grated or shaved
   Parmesan cheese,
salt and freshly ground black pepper
1 tablespoon chopped fresh chives,
   to garnish (optional)

1 Cook the cauliflower in a covered saucepan with a small amount of
   boiling water until just tender – about 10 minutes.

2 Meanwhile, make the cheese sauce by putting the milk, flour and
   margarine into a saucepan. Bring up to the boil, stirring constantly
   with a wire whisk, until the sauce blends and thickens. Reduce
   the heat to low and cook gently, stirring all the time, for another
   30 seconds or so. Add the cheese and mustard to the sauce and
   cook gently for 30 seconds, stirring, until the cheese has melted.
   Season to taste.

3 Preheat the grill. Drain the cauliflower thoroughly, place in a warmed
   ovenproof dish, then pour over the sauce. Sprinkle with the
   Parmesan, then grill until lightly browned. Serve at once, sprinkled
   with fresh chives, if using.

4 POINTS values per serving
16½ POINTS values per recipe

C **219 calories** per serving

Takes **25 minutes**

V

* not recommended

Sage, Onion and Apple Stuffing

Serve these savoury stuffing balls as part of a Sunday roast, or alongside grilled pork chops or chicken for a weekday treat.

Serves 6

100 g (3½ oz) crustless bread
   (about 4 slices)
½ small onion, chopped roughly
1 apple, cored and chopped roughly
1 tablespoon fresh sage, chopped roughly,
   or 1 teaspoon dried sage
4 thick low fat sausages
freshly grated nutmeg
low fat cooking spray
salt and freshly ground black pepper

1½ **POINTS** values per serving
9 **POINTS** values per recipe

C **102 calories** per serving

Takes **15 minutes** to prepare, **25 minutes** to cook.

✻ recommended

1 Preheat the oven to Gas Mark 5/190°C/fan oven 170°C.

2 Tear the bread into rough pieces and place in a food processor. Whizz to coarse crumbs, then add the onion, apple and sage and whizz again until everything is finely chopped.

3 Squeeze the sausages out of their skins and into the processor bowl, add the nutmeg and seasoning, then pulse until the mixture comes together.

4 Shape into 18 stuffing balls and place on a foil-lined baking tray. Lightly mist the stuffing with the cooking spray then bake for 25 minutes until crisp and browned. Serve three balls of stuffing per person.

Leeks with Creamy Cheese Sauce

Enjoy leeks in this lovely recipe – either as a side dish or a light meal.

Serves 2

4 leeks, trimmed and sliced in half
200 g (7 oz) low fat soft cheese
150 ml (5 fl oz) skimmed milk
2 level teaspoons wholegrain mustard
1 tablespoon fresh parsley, chopped
salt and freshly ground black pepper

3 POINTS values per serving
5½ POINTS values per recipe

C **186 calories** per serving

Takes **15 minutes** to prepare,
15 minutes to cook

V

* not recommended

1 Put the leeks into a large saucepan and cover with cold water. Bring to the boil and simmer for 10–12 minutes, until tender.

2 Meanwhile, put the soft cheese into a saucepan and gradually whisk in the milk. Add the wholegrain mustard and parsley. Heat gently, stirring, to make a smooth sauce. Check the seasoning.

3 Preheat a grill to medium hot.

4 Drain the leeks thoroughly. Share between two individual baking dishes. Pour the sauce on top, then grill for 4–5 minutes until browned.

Tip This recipe serves two for a light meal, four as an accompaniment. For an accompaniment, put the leeks into a baking dish, pour the sauce on top, then cover with foil and keep warm in a low oven.

Simple Peppercorn Sauce

Drizzle this creamy sauce over a grilled steak or pork chops – perfection.

Serves 2

low fat cooking spray
2 shallots, chopped finely
100 g (3½ oz) low fat soft cheese
100 ml (3½ fl oz) beef stock
1 teaspoon coarsely crushed peppercorns

1 Spray a non stick frying pan with the cooking spray. Cook the shallots for 3 minutes until softened and golden brown.

2 Blend in the soft cheese, beef stock and peppercorns and simmer for 2 minutes until slightly thickened.

1½ *POINTS* values per serving
2½ *POINTS* values per recipe

60 calories per serving

Takes **10 minutes**

not recommended

All Purpose Gravy

A delicious, all purpose gravy to serve with roasts, chops or bangers and mash.

Serves 4

low fat cooking spray
1 small onion, chopped finely
25 g (1 oz) plain flour
450 ml (16 fl oz) vegetable stock
1 tablespoon soy sauce
1 teaspoon tomato purée
freshly ground black pepper

1 Spray a lidded, non stick frying pan with the cooking spray and cook the onion for 6–7 minutes over a medium heat until browned and softened. Stir in the flour and cook for 2 minutes or until it turns light brown.

2 Gradually blend in the stock, followed by the soy sauce and tomato purée. Bring to the boil, reduce the heat and simmer, covered, for 10 minutes. Season to taste with black pepper.

½ **POINTS** value per serving
1 **POINTS** value per recipe

C **36 calories** per serving

Takes **20 minutes**

V

✱ recommended

Roasted Pepper Salsa

For a taste of summer all year round, spoon this colourful salsa over grilled chicken or fish.

Serves 4

1 red and 1 yellow pepper
100 g (3½ oz) cherry tomatoes, chopped
  roughly
1 tablespoon fresh basil, shredded
2 teaspoons balsamic vinegar
salt and freshly ground black pepper

0 *POINTS* values per serving
0 *POINTS* values per recipe

C **29 calories** per serving

Takes **10 minutes** to prepare + cooling,
25 minutes to cook

V **Vg**

* not recommended

1 Preheat the oven to Gas Mark 6/200°C/fan oven 180°C.

2 Put the peppers in the oven, directly on the oven shelf. Put a piece of foil on the shelf underneath to catch any cooking juices and keep the oven clean. Roast for 20–25 minutes until the peppers are blackened and blistered, then transfer to a bowl, cover and leave to cool.

3 When the peppers are cool enough to handle, peel off the skins, scoop out the seeds, and cut the flesh into ribbons.

4 Mix the roasted peppers back into the juices that will have collected in the bowl, then stir in the tomatoes, basil, balsamic vinegar and add seasoning to taste. Serve at room temperature for the best flavour.

Perfect Poultry

Poultry is so versatile. From stir fries such as Pad Thai Noodles, to delicious meals such as Tarragon Chicken with Lemon Braised Potatoes, there is a dish here to suit all occasions. Make tasty meals for all the family such as Balsamic Roasted Chicken, or try something a little more unusual for a special meal for two, such as Turkey Scallopine with Lemon and Caper Sauce.

For everyday suppers, nothing beats a simple poultry dish

Pad Thai Noodles

These stir fried noodles are a staple Thai dish. They are a great all-in-one meal, incorporating noodles, chicken, prawns and egg, stir fried in a wok with a sweet-sharp sauce, then served topped with a crunchy colourful garnish. Delicious.

Serves 2

100 g (3½ oz) wide rice noodles
low fat cooking spray
100 g (3½ oz) skinless, boneless chicken
     breast, chopped finely
3 shallots, sliced
2 garlic cloves, crushed
¼ teaspoon crushed dried chillies
2 tablespoons Thai fish sauce
1 tablespoon artificial sweetener
juice of a lime
150 g (5½ oz) beansprouts, rinsed
60 g (2 oz) small prawns
1 egg, beaten

For the garnish

2 spring onions, chopped
5 cm (2 inches) cucumber, diced finely
½ red chilli, de-seeded and sliced
2 tablespoons chopped fresh coriander
15 g (½ oz) salted peanuts, chopped finely

5½ **POINTS** values per serving
10½ **POINTS** values per recipe

c   **413 calories** per serving

Takes **25 minutes**

*   not recommended

1 Soak the rice noodles in boiling water for 5 minutes or according to packet instructions, stirring them to separate the strands. Drain and rinse well in cold water.

2 Spray a wok or large non stick frying pan with the cooking spray and heat until smoking. Add the chicken, shallots, garlic and crushed chillies and stir fry for 3 minutes.

3 Mix the fish sauce, sweetener and lime juice together then pour into the pan, quickly followed by the beansprouts and drained noodles. Toss everything together well and cook for 1 minute then stir in the prawns and cook for a further minute.

4 Drizzle the egg over the noodles and leave to set for about 1 minute.

5 Meanwhile, mix the garnish ingredients together then add half to the pan. Give everything one final mix together then serve in warmed bowls, topped with the remainder of the garnish.

Variation For a vegetarian version of Pad Thai, use 150 g (5½ oz) firm tofu, shredded, in place of the chicken and prawns, and use light soy sauce instead of the fish sauce, for 5 **POINTS** values per serving.

Chicken with Cannellini Beans and Rosemary

Serve on its own or with a crisp, zero **POINTS** value green salad.

Serves 2

low fat cooking spray
200 g (7 oz) skinless, boneless chicken breast
    fillets, sliced into small pieces
1 garlic clove, chopped finely
½ teaspoon cumin seeds
a small bunch of rosemary, tough stems
    removed, chopped
zest and juice of ½ a lemon
400 g can cannellini beans, drained
    and rinsed
200 g (7 oz) cherry tomatoes, halved
100 ml (3½ fl oz) vegetable stock
2 tablespoons virtually fat free fromage frais
salt and freshly ground black pepper
a small bunch of parsley or basil, chopped,
    to garnish (optional)

1 Heat a large, lidded non stick frying pan or wok then spray with the cooking spray. Season the chicken and stir fry for 4–5 minutes until golden brown and cooked through.

2 Add the garlic and cumin seeds and stir fry until fragrant. Add the rosemary, lemon zest and juice, cannellini beans, tomatoes, stock and seasoning and stir to combine. Bring to the boil and simmer, covered for 5 minutes.

3 Remove from the heat and allow to cool for a minute or two, then fold in the fromage frais. Serve scattered with parsley or basil, if using.

4½ **POINTS** values per serving
8½ **POINTS** values per recipe

C 275 **calories** per serving

Takes **20 minutes**

✳ not recommended

Turkey Scallopine with Lemon and Caper Sauce

Serve with broccoli for no extra **POINTS** values.

Serves 2

2 x 125 g (4½ oz) turkey breast steaks
zest and juice of ½ a small lemon
low fat cooking spray
1 garlic clove, crushed

150 ml (5 fl oz) chicken stock
2 tablespoons chopped fresh parsley
1 tablespoon baby capers, rinsed
salt and freshly ground black pepper

1 Place each turkey steak between two layers of clingfilm and flatten out to about 5 mm (¼ inch) thick, using a rolling pin or heavy based pan. Press the lemon zest and seasoning into the escalopes.

2 Heat a non stick frying pan, lightly coat with the cooking spray then fry the turkey for 2½ minutes each side. Move to a plate and keep warm.

3 Add the garlic to the pan and fry for a few seconds, without burning, then pour in the chicken stock and lemon juice and bubble fast for 3 minutes until the sauce has reduced by about half. Stir in the parsley and capers. Pour the sauce over the turkey and serve.

2 **POINTS** values per serving
4 **POINTS** values per recipe

137 **calories** per serving

Takes **15 minutes**

* not recommended

Balsamic Roasted Chicken

Serve with 60 g (2 oz) dried pasta such as tagliatelle or linguine per person, cooked according to the packet instructions, for an additional **POINTS** value of 3 per serving.

Serves 4

low fat cooking spray
4 x 150 g (5½ oz) skinless, boneless
   chicken breasts
1 large onion, peeled and quartered
2 red peppers, de-seeded and sliced into
   thin strips
1 green pepper, de-seeded and sliced
   into thin strips
2 garlic cloves, crushed
4 tablespoons balsamic vinegar
100 ml (3½ fl oz) chicken or vegetable stock
a small bunch of fresh or 1 teaspoon dried
   oregano
salt and freshly ground black pepper

2½ **POINTS** values per serving
9½ **POINTS** values per recipe

C   **220 calories** per serving

Takes **10 minutes** to prepare, **25 minutes**
to cook

✱   not recommended

1 Preheat the oven to Gas Mark 4/180°C/fan oven 160°C. Spray a roasting tin with the cooking spray, place the chicken breasts in the tin and season.

2 Spray a large, non stick frying pan with the cooking spray and stir fry the onion for a few minutes, adding a little water to stop it sticking, until it is softened. Add the peppers and garlic, stir fry for a further minute, then tip the mixture over the chicken breasts in the roasting tin.

3 Drizzle over the balsamic vinegar and stock, sprinkle with the herbs, then roast in the oven for 20 minutes or until cooked through. Halfway through spoon some of the sauce over the chicken breasts.

4 Check that the chicken is cooked and serve.

Chicken Kashmiri

Meltingly tender and moist chicken pieces in an aromatic and spicy yogurt sauce. Serve with 150 g (5½ oz) cooked rice per person, for an extra 3 **POINTS** values per serving.

Serves 4

low fat cooking spray
4 x 150 g (5½ oz) skinless, boneless
    chicken breasts, cubed
200 g (7 oz) small new potatoes, quartered
1 onion, chopped finely
4 garlic cloves, crushed
5 cm (2 inch) piece of fresh root ginger,
    peeled and chopped finely
2 cardamom pods, seeds only
½ teaspoons cumin seeds
1 teaspoon ground coriander
1 green chilli, de-seeded and chopped finely
    (optional)
300 ml (10 fl oz) chicken stock
100 g (3½ oz) baby spinach, washed
300 g (10½ oz) low fat natural yogurt
a bunch of fresh coriander, chopped
salt and freshly ground black pepper
4 lemon wedges, to serve

1 Heat a large, lidded, non stick frying pan and spray with the cooking spray. Stir fry the chicken for 4 minutes or so until golden on the edges and white all over. Add the potatoes, onion, garlic, ginger, spices and chilli, if using, and fry for a further 4 minutes until everything is golden.

2 Add the stock, bring to the boil and cover. Simmer gently for 15 minutes until the chicken is tender, the potatoes cooked through and the sauce thickened.

3 Stir in the spinach and check the seasoning. Allow to cool a little and then stir in the yogurt. Scatter with coriander and serve with the lemon wedges.

3½ **POINTS** values per serving
13½ **POINTS** values per recipe

c   **270 calories** per serving

Takes **25 minutes** to prepare,
20 minutes to cook

✱   recommended

Mexican Chicken Tortillas

A fun and satisfying dinner.

Serves 4

8 medium flour tortillas

4 x 150 g (5½ oz) skinless, boneless, chicken breasts, cut into thin strips

150 ml (5 fl oz) low fat natural yogurt

4 medium slices bread, processed to fine breadcrumbs

low fat cooking spray

salt and freshly ground black pepper

For the salsa

500 g (1lb 2 oz) frozen petit pois, cooked and drained

100 g (3½ oz) cherry tomatoes, quartered

1 small red onion, chopped finely

juice of a lime

1 small red chilli, de-seeded and chopped

1 Preheat the oven to Gas Mark 4/180°C/fan oven 160°C. Wrap the tortillas in foil and place in the warm oven to heat through. Meanwhile, place the chicken strips in a bowl and season then add the yogurt and toss until well covered. Place the breadcrumbs on a plate and roll the chicken strips in them.

2 Heat a large non stick frying pan and spray with the cooking spray. Fry the chicken for 4–5 minutes, turning gently until golden brown all over and cooked through.

3 Meanwhile, make the salsa. Place all the ingredients for the salsa in a food processor with some seasoning and blend very briefly to a rough textured paste. Alternatively mash the ingredients together with a fork. Transfer to a bowl.

4 Arrange large spoonfuls of the chicken on the centre of the warmed tortillas and top with the salsa, then roll up and serve.

9½ **POINTS** values per serving
37½ **POINTS** values per recipe

C **690 calories** per serving

Takes **40 minutes**

✳ not recommended

Tarragon Chicken with Lemon Braised Potatoes

An ideal recipe when you want a special meal for two that is really quick to prepare. Add some cooked broccoli florets to complete the meal for no extra *POINTS* values.

Serves 2

300 g (10½ oz) baby new potatoes, halved
300 ml (10 fl oz) chicken or vegetable stock
zest and juice of ½ a lemon
2 tablespoons chopped fresh tarragon
3 tablespoons chopped fresh parsley
2 x 150 g (5½ oz) skinless, boneless chicken
   breasts
low fat cooking spray
16 cherry tomatoes on the vine
¼ teaspoon granulated sugar
salt and freshly ground black pepper

4 *POINTS* values per serving
8 *POINTS* values per recipe

C   300 calories per serving

Takes **10 minutes** to prepare,
25 minutes to cook

* not recommended

1 Preheat the oven to Gas Mark 6/200°C/fan oven 180°C. Place the potatoes in a lidded saucepan with the stock, 1 tablespoon of lemon juice and ½ teaspoon of lemon zest. Bring to the boil and simmer, covered, for 15 minutes until tender.

2 Meanwhile, mix the remaining lemon zest with the tarragon and 2 tablespoons parsley on a plate. Spray the chicken breasts with a little cooking spray and season them lightly. Roll the chicken in the herb mixture to coat completely and place in a roasting tin, sprayed with the cooking spray. Drizzle the rest of the lemon juice over the chicken and cook in the oven for 10 minutes.

3 Add the tomatoes to the roasting tin with the chicken, lightly spray with the cooking spray and sprinkle with the sugar. Return the roasting tin to the oven for 10 minutes, or until the chicken juices run clear when the thickest part of the breast is pierced with a sharp knife or skewer.

4 When the potatoes are tender, remove the lid and increase the heat under the pan. Reduce the liquid for about 10 minutes or until it has almost all evaporated and you are left with about 2 tablespoons of syrupy juices. Toss the potatoes in the juices to glaze and scatter with the remaining parsley. Serve with the chicken and roasted tomatoes.

Variation Replace the chicken breasts with two Quorn fillets for a vegetarian version. This will be 3½ *POINTS* values per serving.

Quick Fruity Chicken Supper

If you've run out of ideas for using leftover chicken, try it in this very tasty, fruity curry with its slightly unusual ingredients and see how well children like it too.

Serves 4

225 g (8 oz) long grain rice
low fat cooking spray
1 small leek or 5 spring onions, finely sliced
350 g (12 oz) skinless roast chicken, chopped
100 ml (3½ fl oz) reduced fat coconut milk
150 ml (5 fl oz) chicken stock
1 tablespoon Jamaican jerk seasoning or
** Thai red curry paste**
210 g can pineapple pieces in natural
** juice, drained**
1 banana, sliced
2 clementines or 1 small orange, segmented
salt and freshly ground black pepper
shredded leek or spring onion, to garnish
** (optional)**

1 Bring a saucepan of water to the boil, add the rice and cook until just tender, about 12 minutes.

2 Meanwhile, spray a wok or non stick frying pan with the cooking spray. Add the leek or spring onions and sauté for 2 minutes. Add the chicken and cook, stirring, for a further 2 minutes.

3 Add the coconut milk, stock and jerk seasoning or Thai curry paste to the chicken mixture. Heat until just boiling, then reduce the heat and simmer, uncovered, for 5–6 minutes.

4 Add the pineapple, banana and clementines or orange to the chicken mixture. Heat through for 2 minutes, then season to taste.

5 Drain the rice and divide between four warmed serving plates. Spoon the chicken mixture on top, then garnish with shredded leek or spring onion, if using. Serve at once.

7 *POINTS* values per serving
28 *POINTS* values per recipe

C   **394 calories** per serving

Takes **25 minutes**

✱   not recommended

Tip Jamaican jerk seasoning tends to be quite hot, so add it according to taste.

Honey and Mustard Chicken Salad

(3 POINTS VALUE)

Serves 4

500 g (1 lb 2 oz) new potatoes, scrubbed and quartered

200 g (7 oz) asparagus, cut into 2.5 cm (1 inch) lengths

2 x 150 g (5½ oz) skinless, boneless chicken breasts

2 teaspoons runny honey

2 tablespoons wholegrain Dijon mustard

low fat cooking spray

1 garlic clove, crushed

a large bunch of watercress

200 g (7 oz) cherry tomatoes, halved

salt and freshly ground black pepper

For the dressing

1 tablespoon wholegrain Dijon mustard

2 tablespoons virtually fat free fromage frais

1 teaspoon runny honey

1 Bring a large, lidded pan of water to the boil, add the potatoes and cook for 15 minutes, or until tender. About 5 minutes before the end of the cooking time, place the asparagus on top and cover the pan. Drain the cooked asparagus and potatoes together.

2 Meanwhile, slice the chicken breasts horizontally to make four thin fillets. Put in a small bowl with the honey, mustard and seasoning and leave for 10 minutes to marinate. Preheat the grill and line the grill pan with foil.

3 Heat a large non stick pan and spray with the cooking spray. Stir fry the garlic for a few seconds then add the potatoes. Season and stir fry for 5 minutes, until browned on the edges. Tip into a large serving bowl.

4 Place the chicken on the grill pan and grill for 4–5 minutes on each side, until cooked through and golden, then slice into strips.

5 Meanwhile in a small bowl, mix together the dressing ingredients with 2 tablespoons of water.

6 Divide the watercress between four serving plates. Add the chicken strips, cherry tomatoes and asparagus to the cooked potatoes and pour over the dressing. Gently fold together and then pile on top of the watercress to serve.

---

3 POINTS values per serving
12 POINTS values per recipe

C **228 calories** per serving

Takes **30 minutes**

* not recommended

Tomato and Turkey Rasher Pizza

This is really quick to prepare and the combination of tomatoes, turkey rashers, cheese and oregano is great.

Serves 2

225 g (8 oz) tomatoes
low fat cooking spray
1 onion, diced finely
1 garlic clove, crushed
1 teaspoon dried oregano
1 x 23 cm (9 inch) ready made thin and
   crispy pizza base
150 g (5½ oz) packet turkey rashers
4 tablespoons grated half fat Cheddar cheese
salt and freshly ground black pepper

---

5 POINTS values per serving
10 POINTS values per recipe

C **348 calories** per serving

Takes **20 minutes** to prepare, **10 minutes** to cook

＊ not recommended

1 Preheat the oven to Gas Mark 7/220°C/fan oven 200°C. Plunge the tomatoes into a large bowl of boiling water for 1 minute until the skins split and then put them straight into a bowl of cold water. Slip off the skins and discard them. Chop the flesh roughly.

2 Spray a saucepan with the cooking spray and heat until sizzling. Add the onion and garlic and cook over a medium heat for 5 minutes until softened. Add the chopped tomatoes and oregano. Reduce the heat and simmer gently for 10 minutes until reduced and thickened. Season.

3 Spread the tomato sauce over the pizza base, top with the turkey rashers and cheese and bake for 10 minutes until golden. Divide in half and serve.

Tip If you don't have time to make a fresh tomato sauce, use 6 tablespoons of passata mixed with the herbs. The **POINTS** values will remain the same.

Creamy Turkey Crêpes

This recipe takes advantage of the ready made crêpes that you can buy from supermarkets. The filling is quick, easy and tasty.

Serves 2

4 ready made crêpes
low fat cooking spray
200 g (7 oz) skinless, boneless turkey fillets, sliced into thin strips
2 tablespoons soy sauce
1 red pepper, de-seeded and sliced finely
2 small courgettes, sliced into thin strips
100 ml (3½ fl oz) vegetable stock
100 g (3½ oz) low fat soft cheese
salt and freshly ground black pepper

1 Preheat the oven to Gas Mark 4/180°C/fan oven 160°C. Wrap the crêpes in foil and place in the warm oven to heat through.

2 Spray a large, non stick frying pan with the cooking spray. Stir fry the turkey strips for 5 minutes, until nearly cooked through and golden.

3 Add the soy sauce, pepper and courgettes. Stir fry for another 2 minutes or until the vegetables begin to soften. Stir in the stock and soft cheese and check the seasoning.

4 Remove the crêpes from the oven and divide the mixture between the warmed crêpes. Roll them up and serve.

6 **POINTS** values per serving
12½ **POINTS** values per recipe

C 530 **calories** per serving

Takes **20 minutes**

* not recommended

Chicken Saltimbocca

The distinctive aromas and flavours of this Italian-inspired chicken dish are utterly sensational. It's the perfect dish for a special occasion. Serve with broccoli or green beans for no extra **POINTS** values.

Serves 2

2 x 150 g (5½ oz) skinless,
  boneless chicken breasts
4 fresh sage leaves or 2 teaspoons
  dried sage
2 thin slices Parma ham
low fat cooking spray
50 ml (2 fl oz) sweet sherry or Marsala
100 ml (3½ fl oz) chicken or
  vegetable stock
salt and freshly ground black pepper

1 Place the chicken breasts, well spaced, on a large piece of clingfilm. Cover with a second piece of clingfilm. Using a meat mallet or frying pan, gently but firmly beat out the chicken breasts until flattened and an even thickness.

2 Remove the clingfilm and place two sage leaves or 1 teaspoon of dried sage on top of each chicken breast. Season, then place a slice of Parma ham on top of each one. Turn the chicken breasts over, then roll them up from the narrow end. The ham should be on the outside. Secure with cocktail sticks.

3 Spray a heavy based, lidded frying pan with the cooking spray. Add the chicken rolls and cook over a medium-high heat for about 2–3 minutes, turning often to seal. Pour in the sweet sherry or Marsala, allow it to bubble up, then add the stock. Heat until simmering, then cover with a lid or piece of foil and turn the heat to low.

4 Simmer for 20–25 minutes, spooning the juices over the chicken after 15 minutes. Remove the cocktail sticks before serving.

3½ **POINTS** values per serving
7 **POINTS** values per recipe

C   **224 calories** per serving

Takes **15 minutes** to prepare,
30 minutes to cook

✱   not recommended

Tip Check that the chicken is cooked by piercing with a sharp knife – the juices should run clear.

Oriental Duck Salad

The flavours, colours and textures in this Asian-style salad are simply sensational. You'll love it.

Serves 4

2 x 150 g (5½ oz) skinless, boneless duck breasts

1 red, green or yellow pepper, de-seeded and thinly sliced

a bunch of spring onions, sliced thinly

100 g (3½ oz) radishes, sliced thinly

1 carrot, pared into strips

2 pak choi, leaves separated

150 g (5½ oz) beansprouts

1 tablespoon chopped fresh coriander

¼ lemongrass stem, chopped finely

1 ripe mango (300 g/10½ oz), de-stoned, peeled and chopped

½ fresh red chilli, de-seeded

2 teaspoons fresh grated ginger

juice of ½ a lime

1 tablespoon soy sauce

2 POINTS values per serving
8 POINTS values per recipe

170 calories per serving

Takes **15 minutes** to prepare, **35 minutes** to cook

✱ not recommended

1 Preheat the oven to Gas Mark 6/200°C/fan oven 180°C. Put the duck breasts into a roasting pan and roast for 20–25 minutes, or until cooked through. Cover and leave to rest for 10 minutes.

2 Meanwhile, in a large salad bowl, mix together the pepper, spring onions, radishes, carrot, pak choi, beansprouts, coriander and lemongrass.

3 Put the mango, chilli, ginger and lime juice into a blender, or use a hand blender, and blend until smooth. Add 2–3 tablespoons of cold water to thin the consistency if it is too thick.

4 Just before serving, slice the duck breasts. Add the soy sauce to the salad, tossing to coat. Serve the salad on four plates, topped with the sliced duck and drizzled with the mango dressing.

Variation Substitute baby spinach or Chinese leaves if you can't find pak choi, for the same **POINTS** values.

Marvellous Meat

For fast, easy dinners during the week, try Warm Spicy Sausage and Spinach Salad, Lamb Brochettes with Honey and Lemon or Spicy Chorizo Farfalle. For a classy supper party give Steak with Sweet and Sour Onions a go.

Enjoy an evening meal together with some satisfying meat ideas

Parma Ham and Artichoke Pizza

Parma ham – a classic Italian salted and air-dried meat – is wonderfully tasty and crisps up like thin bacon on top of pizza. Tinned artichokes are delicious, easy to use and available in most supermarkets – even better, they have a **POINTS** value of zero.

Serves 4

low fat cooking spray
144 g packet pizza base mix
4 tablespoons sun-dried tomato purée
400 g can artichokes, drained and halved
   if large
8 sage leaves or 2 teaspoons dried sage
6 thin slices Parma ham
2 teaspoons olive oil

4½ **POINTS** values per serving
17½ **POINTS** values per recipe

C   **273 calories** per serving

Takes **30 minutes** to prepare,
20 minutes to cook

* not recommended

1 Preheat the oven to Gas Mark 7/ 220°C/fan oven 200°C. Spray a baking sheet with the cooking spray.

2 To make the pizza base, empty the contents of the sachet into a bowl and follow the packet instructions to make one large pizza approximately 20 cm (8 inch) in diameter.

3 Spread the sun-dried tomato purée over the pizza base, top with the artichokes, sprinkle over the sage leaves or dried sage and top with the Parma ham. Drizzle with the olive oil. Bake for 15–20 minutes until the base is golden and the ham crispy.

Tip If you prefer your Parma ham soft, put it on after the pizza is cooked.

Variation For a veggie version, omit the ham, reduce the sun-dried tomato purée to 2 tablespoons, mix with 2 tablespoons of ordinary tomato purée and add 125 g (4½ oz) light mozzarella, drained and sliced, for 5 **POINTS** values per serving.

Beef Stroganoff for Two

Serve this rich stew with 100 g (3½ oz) boiled potatoes per person and a peppery watercress or rocket and tomato salad, drizzled with balsamic vinegar for 1 extra *POINTS* value per serving.

Serves 2

low fat cooking spray
2 shallots, chopped
2 garlic cloves, sliced finely
2 x 150 g (5½ oz) rump or entrecôte steaks, each 2.5 cm (1 inch) thick, all fat removed and meat sliced thinly
200 g (7 oz) chestnut mushrooms, sliced
100 ml (3½ fl oz) vegetable or beef stock
4 tablespoons very low fat fromage frais
salt and freshly ground black pepper

1 Heat a large, non stick frying pan and spray with the cooking spray. Stir fry the shallots and garlic for 5 minutes or until softened, adding a little water if necessary to prevent them from sticking.

2 Add the steak and mushrooms and season. Stir fry on a high heat for 2–3 minutes, until the meat is browned all over.

3 With the heat still turned up high, quickly add the stock and bubble for a few seconds, scraping up any bits stuck to the bottom of the pan with a wooden spatula.

4 Turn the heat off, allow to cool for a minute, then stir in the fromage frais and serve.

4 *POINTS* values per serving
8 *POINTS* values per recipe

225 calories per serving

Takes **25 minutes**

not recommended

Pork with 5 Spice Plums

There's more than a hint of the Orient to this pan fried pork dish. A medium portion (40 g/1½ oz) of egg noodles per person makes an ideal accompaniment, for an extra 2 **POINTS** values per serving.

Serves 2

1 level tablespoon cornflour
½ teaspoon Chinese 5 spice powder
300 g (10½ oz) extra lean pork fillet, cut into
    15 mm (⅝ inch) slices
low fat cooking spray
1 tablespoon soy sauce
150 ml (5 fl oz) apple juice
1 garlic clove, crushed
2 tablespoons medium sherry
2 plums, stoned and each cut into six wedges
1 teaspoon redcurrant jelly

1 Mix the cornflour and 5 spice powder together and dip the pork in to coat lightly.

2 Spray a non stick frying pan with the cooking spray, add the pork, and fry for 2–3 minutes each side until browned.

3 Meanwhile, blend the remaining spiced cornflour with the soy sauce, apple juice and 3 tablespoons of cold water, then set aside.

4 Add the garlic to the pan with the pork and fry for 30 seconds without burning, then pour in the sherry and bubble briefly.

5 Add the sauce mixture to the pan, add the plums and redcurrant jelly and simmer for 3 minutes, then serve.

5½ **POINTS** values per serving
11½ **POINTS** values per recipe

C 282 **calories** per serving

Takes **20 minutes**

* not recommended

Tip If you cannot find fresh plums or they are out of season, use canned plums in their juice instead.

Ham and Leek Rolls in Parsley Sauce

This is a lovely warming and satisfying farmhouse style supper dish. A golden, bubbling topping reveals a creamy leek and ham mixture underneath – absolutely delicious. Serve with 100 g (3½ oz) new potatoes and green beans per person, for 1 extra **POINTS** value per serving.

Serves 4

4 thick leeks
2 teaspoons cornflour
300 ml (10 fl oz) skimmed milk
2 tablespoons chopped fresh parsley
1 teaspoon low fat polyunsaturated
     margarine
4 x 25 g slices lean ham
2 tablespoons grated half fat Cheddar cheese
1 tomato, quartered, de-seeded and chopped
salt and freshly ground black pepper

1½ **POINTS** value per serving
5½ **POINTS** values per recipe

C   120 calories per serving

Takes **15 minutes** to prepare,
15 minutes to cook

∗   not recommended

1 Trim the roots and dark green stems of the leeks so you end up with lengths of about 17 cm (6½ inches). Blanch them in boiling water for 5 minutes. Drain them well and pat dry with kitchen paper.

2 Blend the cornflour with 2 tablespoons of the milk to form a paste. Put the rest of the milk in a saucepan and bring it to the boil. When the milk starts to bubble take the pan off the heat and stir in the cornflour paste. Return the pan to the heat and simmer, stirring, for about 1 minute until the sauce thickens.

3 Stir the parsley, margarine and seasoning into the sauce.

4 Preheat the oven to Gas Mark 6/200°C/fan oven 180°C. Wrap each leek in a slice of ham. Place the leek and ham rolls in a shallow dish with the join of the ham facing downwards. Pour over the sauce.

5 Mix the cheese with the chopped tomato and scatter this over the top. Bake for 15 minutes until the topping is golden and bubbling. Serve on four warmed plates.

Variation Try canned celery hearts, drained, instead of fresh leeks, for the same **POINTS** values.

Moroccan Lamb Tagine

Serve with 150 g (5½ oz) cooked couscous per person, stirred through with a handful or two of fresh mint or coriander, or both, for an additional 2½ *POINTS* values per serving.

Serves 4

low fat cooking spray
600 g (1 lb 5 oz) lean lamb steaks, all fat removed and diced
2 onions, chopped
3 garlic cloves, crushed
500 g (1 lb 2 oz) butternut or acorn squash, peeled, de-seeded and diced
400 g can chick peas, drained
400 g can chopped tomatoes
200 g can apricots in natural juice, drained but keep the juice and chop the apricots
425 ml (15 fl oz) vegetable or lamb stock
a pinch of saffron strands (or 1 teaspoon ground turmeric)
2 cinnamon sticks
2 tablespoons coriander seeds, crushed
½ teaspoon dried chilli flakes
salt and freshly ground black pepper
handful of fresh coriander to garnish, optional

1 Spray a large, lidded non stick pan with the cooking spray and brown the lamb, seasoning as you go. You may need to do this in batches. Remove all the lamb to a plate.

2 Add the onions and garlic to the pan with 100 ml (3½ fl oz) of water, and stir fry until softened. Scrape up any bits from the bottom of the pan. Return all the meat to the pan and add all the other ingredients. Stir, cover and leave to simmer for 30 minutes.

3 Remove the lid and boil the tagine for a few minutes if necessary to thicken the sauce. Season to taste, then garnish with the coriander, if using.

5 *POINTS* values per serving
19 *POINTS* values per recipe

C 348 calories per serving

Takes **20 minutes** to prepare, **30 minutes** to cook

✳ recommended

Variation This dish is also good made with the same quantity of rump beef steaks rather than lamb, for 4½ *POINTS* values per serving.

Lamb and Sweet Potato Casserole

You'll love the flavours of this delicious spiced lamb casserole – it's perfect for chilly winter weather.

Serves 4

low fat cooking spray
450 g (1 lb) lean lamb leg steak, trimmed of fat
   and cut into chunks
2 large red onions, thinly sliced
2 garlic cloves, crushed
1 teaspoon ground coriander
8 green cardamom pods, split open
600 g (1 lb 5 oz) sweet potatoes, peeled and cut
   into large chunks
425 ml (15 fl oz) vegetable or chicken stock
salt and freshly ground black pepper

1 Preheat the oven to Gas Mark 4/180°C/fan oven 160°C.

2 Spray a large, lidded, flameproof casserole dish with the cooking spray and heat until hot. Add the lamb chunks and cook until browned. Add the onions and garlic. Cook for 3–4 minutes, stirring, until softened.

3 Add the ground coriander, cardamom pods and sweet potatoes to the casserole. Pour in the stock. Season.

4 Transfer to the oven and cook for 1½ hours, or until the meat is tender. Serve.

4½ *POINTS* values per serving
18 *POINTS* values per recipe

286 **calories** per serving

Takes **15 minutes** to prepare,
1½ **hours** to cook

✱ recommended

Lamb Brochettes with Honey and Lemon

Serve in a pitta bread per person, for an extra 2½ **POINTS** values per serving, or with 150 g (5½ oz) cooked rice per person, for an extra 3 **POINTS** values per serving.

Serves 4

400 g (14 oz) lean lamb leg steaks, trimmed of fat and cut into 8 strips
2 lemons, each cut into quarter wedges
1 tablespoon clear honey, heated
salt and freshly ground black pepper

For the marinade
150 ml (5 fl oz) low fat natural yogurt
4 garlic cloves, crushed
a small bunch of fresh mint, chopped

3 **POINTS** values per serving
12 **POINTS** values per recipe

C 225 calories per serving

Takes **30 minutes** + **1–12 hours** marinating

✱ not recommended

1 Thread the lamb strips on to eight pre-soaked wooden skewers. In a tray long enough to accommodate the skewers lying down, mix together the marinade of yogurt, garlic, mint and seasoning.

2 Put the meat in the marinade and turn until well coated. Cover and leave to marinate for at least 1 hour but preferably overnight in the refrigerator.

3 Heat the grill to high and transfer the skewers on to the grill tray. Arrange the lemon wedges around the meat and brush the brochettes with the warm honey.

4 Grill for 4 minutes then turn the brochettes and lemon. Spoon any remaining marinade over the lamb and brush the lemon with honey again. Grill again for another 4 minutes or until the lamb is just cooked through.

Tip The wooden skewers should be soaked in water for 10 minutes before use to prevent them from burning.

Pasta with Sausage and Mustard Sauce

A lovely, easy meal that is sure to warm and soothe on an autumnal evening. Serve with roasted red peppers tossed with garlic, balsamic vinegar and seasoning, for no extra **POINTS** values.

Serves 4

175 g (6 oz) spaghetti
low fat cooking spray
2 garlic cloves, chopped finely
400 g (14 oz) low fat sausages, sliced
    diagonally
100 ml (3½ fl oz) white wine
100 ml (3½ fl oz) vegetable stock
2 tablespoons Dijon or wholegrain mustard
85 g bag of watercress or baby spinach,
    shredded
4 tablespoons half fat crème fraîche
a small bunch of fresh parsley, thyme or
    oregano, tough stems removed, leaves
    chopped, plus extra to garnish
salt and freshly ground black pepper

7 POINTS values per serving
28½ POINTS values per recipe

C **404 calories** per serving

Takes **35 minutes** to prepare,
15 minutes to cook

✻ not recommended

1 Bring a saucepan of water to the boil, add the pasta and cook for 5 minutes or according to the packet instructions, until al dente.

2 Meanwhile, heat a large, non stick frying pan, spray with the cooking spray and then stir fry the garlic for 30 seconds. Add the sausages and stir fry on a medium heat for 5–10 minutes, until they are browned all over.

3 Turn up the heat, add the wine and then bubble for a few seconds before adding the stock, mustard and watercress or spinach. Mix thoroughly and then simmer for 5 minutes. Turn off the heat and stir in the crème fraîche and herbs.

4 Drain the pasta but retain a little of the cooking liquid and add it to the sauce. This will help the sauce to stick to the pasta. Toss it all together, season and serve, garnished with the reserved herb of your choice.

Beef Teriyaki Skewers with Stir Fry Vegetables

An exotic twist to beef.

Serves 4

350 g (12 oz) fillet beef steak, cut into strips
2 tablespoons teriyaki sauce
1 small onion, quartered and separated
  into layers
low fat cooking spray
1 red, green or yellow pepper, de-seeded and
  chopped into matchsticks
100 g (3½ oz) mange tout, trimmed
2 teaspoons light soy sauce
4 teaspoons sherry
salt and freshly ground black pepper

1 Coat the steak with the teriyaki sauce in a shallow dish. Stir in the onion and leave to marinate for 30 minutes.

2 Preheat the grill to a medium hot setting. Thread the steak on to four wooden or metal skewers and place on a grill pan. Reserve the onion.

3 Grill for 7–8 minutes, turning halfway through the cooking time. Add a couple more minutes if you prefer your beef well done.

4 Meanwhile, spray a non stick wok or frying pan with cooking spray. Add the onion, pepper and mange tout and stir fry for 2–3 minutes, or until just starting to soften. Stir in the soy sauce and sherry. Check the seasoning.

5 Divide the vegetables between warmed plates and place the skewers on top. Serve at once.

2½ **POINTS** values per serving
10 **POINTS** values per recipe

C **177 calories** per serving

Takes **15 minutes** + **30 minutes** marinating

✱ not recommended

Tip If using wooden skewers, they should be soaked in water for 10 minutes before use to prevent them from burning. Alternatively you can cover the tips with aluminium foil.

Warm Spicy Sausage and Spinach Salad

This delicious warm salad is perfect at the end of summer when tomatoes are at their sweetest.

Serves 2

4 thick low fat sausages
150 g (5½ oz) cherry tomatoes
225 g (8 oz) baby spinach, washed
salt and freshly ground black pepper

For the dressing
1 tablespoon balsamic vinegar

1 small red chilli, de-seeded and
chopped finely or ¼ teaspoon
dried chilli flakes
1 small garlic clove, crushed
2 teaspoons olive oil

1 Preheat the oven to Gas Mark 7/220°C/fan oven 200°C. Place the sausages and tomatoes in a roasting tin. Season and bake for 15–20 minutes, shaking the tin occasionally, until the sausages are browned and the tomatoes softened. Once the sausages are cooked, slice them diagonally into bite sized pieces.

2 Mix together the dressing ingredients in a medium size bowl and add the spinach. Season, then toss together. Divide between two serving plates. Spoon the hot tomatoes and sausage slices on top and serve.

3½ **POINTS** values per serving
7 **POINTS** values per recipe

c   **292 calories** per serving

Takes **10 minutes** to prepare,
20 minutes to cook

*   not recommended

Cajun Pork Steaks with Sweet Potato Chips

If you're looking for something different to serve next time you have friends around for dinner, this recipe will prove a talking point. The tropical flavours of the salsa perfectly complement the spicy pork steaks and caramelised sweet potato chips.

Serves 4

low fat cooking spray
1.25 kg (2 lb 12 oz) sweet potatoes, peeled and cut into wedges
½ vegetable stock cube
4 x 175 g (6 oz) pork loin steaks, trimmed of all fat
juice of a lime and zest of ½ a lime
2 teaspoons Cajun spice powder
½ pineapple, peeled, cored and chopped finely
½ red pepper, de-seeded and diced
½ green chilli, de-seeded and diced

---

8 POINTS values per serving
31½ POINTS values per recipe

C **524 calories** per serving

Takes **25 minutes** to prepare, **30 minutes** to cook

✱ not recommended

1 Preheat the oven to Gas Mark 6/200°C/fan oven 180°C. Lightly spray a baking tray with the cooking spray.

2 Cook the sweet potato wedges in boiling water with the vegetable stock cube for 5 minutes. Drain the potatoes, spread out on the baking tray and spray with the cooking spray. Cook in the oven for 25–30 minutes, turning half way through.

3 Pat the pork steaks dry on kitchen towel. Place on a plate, drizzle half the lime juice over them and sprinkle the Cajun spice on both sides of each steak. Set aside. Grill to medium high.

4 Mix the remaining lime juice and zest together with the pineapple, pepper and chilli in a small serving bowl.

5 Grill the pork steaks for 12–15 minutes, or until they are cooked through and the juices run clear. Serve with the sweet potato chips and the pineapple salsa spooned over the pork.

Tip To prepare a pineapple, firstly slice off the base and the leaves of the pineapple. Stand the pineapple upright and cut into wedges. Trim away the core from each wedge, and then slice the flesh away from the skin, as if you were preparing a melon.

Steak with Sweet and Sour Onions

The tangy sweet and sour onions make a delicious accompaniment to steak and creamy mashed potatoes enhanced with horseradish.

Serves 2

500 g (1 lb 2 oz) potatoes, peeled and chopped roughly
low fat cooking spray
1 large onion, sliced
3 tablespoons sherry vinegar
250 ml (9 fl oz) beef stock
1½ teaspoons granulated artificial sweetener
2 x 125 g (4½ oz) sirloin steaks
4 tablespoons skimmed milk, warmed
1½ tablespoons horseradish sauce
salt and freshly ground black pepper

---

6 POINTS values per serving
12½ POINTS values per recipe

C **420 calories** per serving

Takes **30 minutes**

* not recommended

1 Bring a saucepan of water to the boil, add the potatoes and cook for 20 minutes, or until tender.

2 Meanwhile, spray a non stick frying pan with the cooking spray and fry the onion for 5–6 minutes until browned, adding a splash of stock if needed to stop the onions sticking.

3 Add the sherry vinegar, stock and sweetener to the browned onions, season and simmer uncovered for 10 minutes until tender and syrupy.

4 Heat another non stick frying pan, season the steaks, and spray with the cooking spray. Cook for 3 minutes each side for medium steaks.

5 When the potatoes are tender, drain into a colander, return to the pan and mash.

6 Mix in the warmed milk, horseradish sauce and seasoning to the potatoes. Serve alongside the steak, with the sweet and sour onions spooned over.

Tip For the best possible texture for mashed potatoes, use a potato ricer.

Tandoori Lamb with Warm Rice Salad

The lamb in this recipe could be cooked on a barbecue for that unique, smoky flavour.

Serves 4

300 g (10½ oz) low fat natural yogurt
2 garlic cloves, crushed
2.5 cm (1 inch) piece of fresh root ginger,
    grated finely
2 teaspoons ground turmeric
2 teaspoons garam masala
2 teaspoons ground coriander
400 g (14 oz) lean lamb fillets
200 g (7 oz) rice
juice of a lemon
a small bunch of coriander, chopped
a small bunch of mint, chopped
a bunch of spring onions, chopped finely
100 g (3½ oz) mixed salad and herb leaves
4 ripe tomatoes, diced
salt and freshly ground black pepper

1 Mix together the yogurt, garlic, ginger, turmeric, garam masala and ground coriander and then toss the lamb in this mixture to coat thoroughly. Cover and chill for at least 5 minutes, but overnight is preferable.

2 Bring a pan of water to the boil and cook the rice according to the instructions on the packet.

3 Preheat the grill to medium high and line the grill pan with foil. Grill the lamb for 5–7 minutes on each side, until just cooked through and browned. Remove to a plate, cover with foil and allow to rest for a few minutes.

4 Meanwhile, drain the cooked rice and mix with the lemon juice, herbs, spring onions, salad leaves, tomatoes and seasoning. Cut the lamb into slices and serve warm with the rice salad.

9 *POINTS* values per serving
36 *POINTS* values per recipe

C 380 calories per serving

Takes 20 minutes + marinating

* not recommended

Spicy Chorizo Farfalle

For a quick and easy supper that the whole family will love, try this spicy and tasty pasta dish.

Serves 4

150 g (5½ oz) chorizo sausage, sliced
1 red pepper, de-seeded and sliced
1 green pepper, de-seeded and sliced
1 yellow pepper, de-seeded and sliced

500 g (1 lb 2 oz) passata
150 g (5½ oz) farfalle
185 g can black olives in brine, drained

1 Heat a large non stick frying pan and dry fry the chorizo and peppers for 3–5 minutes until beginning to brown. Add the passata and simmer for 10 minutes, adding a little water if the sauce gets too thick.

2 Meanwhile, bring a large pan of water to the boil, add the pasta and cook according to the packet instructions. Drain.

3 Toss the olives with the pasta and serve with the sauce on top.

5 *POINTS* values per serving
20½ *POINTS* values per recipe

C 316 calories per recipe

Takes 25 minutes

* not recommended

Braised Steak with Mushrooms and Shallots

Simple – and simply delicious. This dish makes quite a classy choice for a supper party. Serve with plenty of fresh vegetables, such as broccoli, for a very satisfying meal and no additional **POINTS** values.

Serves 4

low fat cooking spray
500 g (1 lb 2 oz) lean beef fillet steak,
   in four large pieces
350 g (12 oz) shallots
225 g (8 oz) mushrooms, halved
850 ml (1½ pints) beef stock
1 bay leaf
1 tablespoon wholegrain mustard
2 tablespoons Worcestershire sauce
salt and freshly ground black pepper

3½ **POINTS** values per serving
13½ **POINTS** values per recipe

C   **236 calories** per serving

Takes **20 minutes** to prepare,
2 hours to cook

✱   not recommended

1 Preheat the oven to Gas Mark 4/180°C/fan oven 160°C.

2 Spray a flameproof, lidded casserole dish with the cooking spray and heat on the hob. Add the pieces of steak. Cook over a high heat, turning once, until sealed and browned – about 2–3 minutes. You may need to do this in batches.

3 Return all the beef to the casserole dish and add the shallots, mushrooms, stock and bay leaf. Bring up to the boil, then stir in the mustard and Worcestershire sauce. Season and cover with the lid.

4 Transfer to the oven and cook for 2 hours, until the meat is very tender. Remove the bay leaf and serve.

Fantastic Fish

If you want your family to eat more fish and seafood, try some of these fabulous dishes, such as Tuna with Spring Vegetable Sauté. Seafood Pasta Shells and Chinese Prawns take hardly any time at all and are bound to go down well, and everyone will love Ligurian Pizza.

Fresh fish is so good for you and makes a tasty fast supper

Salmon, Mussel and Noodle Stew

This easy fish dish tastes superb and you can cook it all in one pan.

Serves 4

1 large leek, trimmed and sliced

a bunch of spring onions, trimmed and sliced finely

1 garlic clove, chopped finely

600 ml (1 pint) vegetable stock

50 g (1¾ oz) vermicelli or thread egg noodles

175 g (6 oz) salmon fillet

450 g (1 lb) mussels in shells, scrubbed

150 ml (5 fl oz) skimmed milk

salt and freshly ground black pepper

2 tablespoons chopped flat leaf parsley, to serve

---

2 *POINTS* values per serving
8½ *POINTS* values per recipe

195 **calories** per serving

Takes **10 minutes** to prepare,
20 minutes to cook

✱ not recommended.

1 Put the leek, spring onions, garlic and stock into a large, lidded, saucepan. Bring to the boil, reduce the heat and simmer for 5 minutes.

2 Add the vermicelli or egg noodles and sit the whole salmon fillet on top. Cover and cook gently for 5 minutes. Lift the salmon from the pan and leave to cool for a few minutes.

3 Meanwhile, check the mussels, discarding any that are damaged or remain open when tapped. Add the mussels to the saucepan. Cover and simmer for 2–3 minutes until the shells open (discard any that remain shut).

4 Flake the salmon, discarding the skin and any bones. Return to the saucepan with the milk and reheat gently. Season to taste then serve, sprinkled with parsley.

Tuna Burgers with Cucumber Relish

Canned tuna is a great store cupboard standby that's put to good use in these appetising burgers. Serve with a zero **POINTS** value mixed leaf salad.

Serves 2

1 egg, beaten
2 tablespoons chopped fresh coriander
1 tablespoon sweet chilli sauce
1 spring onion, chopped finely
200 g can tuna in brine, drained and flaked
60 g (2 oz) fresh breadcrumbs
low fat cooking spray
salt and freshly ground black pepper

To serve

60 g (2 oz) cucumber, diced
¼ yellow pepper, de-seeded and diced
2 teaspoons seasoned rice vinegar
2 English muffins, split
2 lettuce leaves

1 In a bowl, mix the egg with the coriander, chilli sauce and spring onion then stir in the flaked tuna, breadcrumbs and seasoning.

2 Mix together well and shape into two burgers, using damp hands to stop the mixture sticking.

3 Lightly coat a non stick frying pan with the cooking spray. Fry the burgers for 4 minutes on each side, until hot, crisp and golden brown.

4 Meanwhile, mix the diced cucumber and pepper with the seasoned rice vinegar to make a crunchy relish.

5 Lightly toast the English muffins and place half a muffin on each plate. Sit the burgers on the muffins, with a lettuce leaf tucked underneath. Spoon over the relish and top with the remaining muffin halves. Serve immediately.

5½ **POINTS** values per serving
11 **POINTS** values per recipe

C 379 **calories** per serving

Takes **15 minutes**

✻ recommended (burgers only)

Provençal Trout Parcels

This is a recipe from the south of France. It uses a lot of garlic, which mellows in flavour as it bakes.

Serves 2

2 shallots, chopped finely

2 x 250 g (9 oz) trouts, scaled and gutted but heads left on

4 tomatoes, skinned, de-seeded and chopped

4 garlic cloves, crushed

¼ teaspoon fennel seeds, crushed in a mortar or with a knife

a few sprigs of fresh thyme, woody stems removed

a few sprigs of fresh rosemary, woody stems removed

salt and freshly ground black pepper

a small bunch of chopped fresh parsley, to garnish

1 Preheat the oven to Gas Mark 4/180°C/fan oven 160°C and prepare two large squares of non stick baking parchment big enough to parcel up the fish.

2 Place the shallots in the cavities of the fish and then place each fish on a square of parchment. Sprinkle over all the other ingredients, except the parsley. Season and fold up the parchment to enclose the fish completely, so that no steam can escape.

3 Place the wrapped fish on a baking tray and bake for 20–25 minutes until cooked through.

4 Serve the parsley in a small bowl on the table to garnish.

5½ *POINTS* values per serving
10½ *POINTS* values per recipe

174 calories per serving

Takes **15 minutes** to prepare, **25 minutes** to cook

not recommended

Tip To skin tomatoes easily, put the tomatoes in a bowl and cover with boiling water. Leave for about 10 seconds, then remove with a slotted spoon. Cool under cold water and the skin should peel off easily. If it doesn't, then return the tomatoes to the hot water for about 5 seconds then try to peel them again and use according to the recipe. This method of preparation is also perfect for preparing tomatoes for including in salsas.

Chinese Prawns

This will be on the table in less time than it takes to go for a take away and tastes wonderful.

Serves 2

150 g (5½ oz) rice
low fat cooking spray
200 g (7 oz) baby leeks
150 ml (5 fl oz) chicken stock
2 teaspoons fresh root ginger, grated or
    chopped finely
1 tablespoon sherry vinegar or red wine
    vinegar
1 tablespoon soy sauce
175 g (6 oz) peeled prawns, raw if possible
75 g (2¾ oz) spinach

5 POINTS values per serving
10 POINTS values per recipe

C   **353 calories** per serving

Takes **25 minutes**

＊   not recommended

1 Bring a saucepan of water to the boil, add the rice, bring back to the boil and simmer gently for 20 minutes.

2 About 10 minutes before the rice will be ready, spray a large wok or frying pan with the cooking spray and heat to a medium heat. Once hot, stir fry the whole baby leeks for 2–3 minutes until browned and softened.

3 Turn the heat down to low and add the chicken stock, ginger, vinegar and soy sauce. Simmer for another 2–3 minutes.

4 If using raw prawns, add them to the wok and cook them for 2–3 minutes or until they have changed to a pink colour all over. Cooked prawns will just need 1 minute to heat through.

5 Meanwhile, drain the rice, rinse with boiling water, drain again and share between two warmed plates. Add the spinach to the prawns and sauce, stir in until wilted then serve immediately with the rice.

Variation Use spring onions instead of the baby leeks or you can substitute pak choi or Chinese leaves for the spinach. Chinese leaves will take a little longer to cook, so add them when you add the raw prawns. The **POINTS** values remain the same.

Crab with Courgette 'Linguini'

This fresh and vibrant dish will satisfy your tastebuds and your appetite. This works well hot or cold – as a starter or main course. Try using the courgette 'linguini' instead of the pasta in other pasta dishes too.

Serves 2

low fat cooking spray
2 garlic cloves, crushed
1 red chilli, de-seeded and chopped finely
zest and juice of a lemon
400 g (14 oz) courgettes, sliced into ribbons
170 g can cooked white crabmeat or
   fresh white crabmeat, drained
a small bunch of coriander or parsley, chopped
salt and freshly ground black pepper

1 Heat a large non stick frying pan and spray with the cooking spray. Fry the garlic for 1–2 minutes, until just golden.

2 Add the chilli, lemon zest and courgettes and stir fry for 3–4 minutes, until just softened. Gently fold in the crabmeat, lemon juice, fresh coriander or parsley and seasoning, and serve.

1 **POINTS** value per serving
2 **POINTS** values per recipe

C **100 calories** per serving

Takes **30 minutes**

* not recommended

Caribbean Cod

Jazz up some fresh fish with this zingy pineapple salsa.

Serves 4

4 x 150 g (5½ oz) cod steaks or
   fillets
low fat cooking spray

For the salsa

1 small red onion, chopped finely
1 green chilli, de-seeded and
   chopped finely
1 red pepper, de-seeded and diced

a handful of basil leaves, chopped
   finely
juice of 2 limes
2 tomatoes, de-seeded and chopped
   finely
2 slices of fresh pineapple, peeled,
   cored and diced
salt (optional)

1 Make the salsa by combining together all the salsa ingredients in a bowl. Add salt if necessary, cover and leave to one side. If you do this in a food processor, do not over process or you will lose the chunky texture of the fish.

2 Preheat the grill to a medium heat.

3 Spray the cod steaks with the cooking spray and grill them for 3–4 minutes on each side, or until just cooked through. Spoon the salsa over the cod and serve immediately.

2 **POINTS** values per serving
8 **POINTS** values per recipe

174 **calories** per serving

Takes **20 minutes**

* not recommended

Tuna with Spring Vegetable Sauté

Full of goodness, this mixture of fresh spring vegetables and grilled tuna is bursting with flavour.

Serves 4

4 x 140 g (5 oz) tuna steaks
3 tablespoons soy sauce
juice of a lemon
1 teaspoon ground ginger
low fat cooking spray
3 shallots, diced
150 g (5½ oz) green beans, trimmed
100 g (3½ oz) baby carrots, peeled
50 g (1¾ oz) baby courgettes, halved
   lengthways
50 g (1¾ oz) cherry tomatoes
150 ml (5 fl oz) vegetable stock
salt and freshly ground black pepper

---

3 POINTS values per serving
12½ POINTS values per recipe

196 calories per serving

Takes **20 minutes**

✱ not recommended

1 Place the tuna steaks in a non metallic bowl.

2 Mix together the soy sauce, lemon juice, black pepper and ground ginger and pour this over the tuna steaks. Cover and leave to marinate for 10–15 minutes.

3 Meanwhile, heat a large, non stick frying pan and spray with the cooking spray. Add the vegetables, except the cherry tomatoes, and stir fry for 5–6 minutes until they start to brown in places.

4 Add the tomatoes and pour in the vegetable stock. Cook over a very high heat so the stock is bubbling well. Season and cook for 6–8 minutes, stirring occasionally.

5 Meanwhile, heat a griddle pan or non stick frying pan and spray with the cooking spray. Remove the tuna steaks from the marinade. Cook for 5–6 minutes on each side, depending on how well cooked you like your fish.

6 Serve the tuna steaks on a bed of the vegetables with a little of the sauce poured over the top.

Smoked Haddock and New Potatoes in Mustard Sauce

A robust, vibrantly flavoured supper that's quick and easy to prepare in one pan.

Serves 2

200 g (7 oz) new potatoes, halved
200 g (7 oz) smoked haddock fillet
low fat cooking spray
4 leeks, sliced finely
2 teaspoons wholegrain Dijon mustard
200 g (7 oz) virtually fat free fromage frais
juice of ½ a lemon
a small bunch of fresh tarragon or parsley,
**   chopped finely (optional)**
salt and freshly ground black pepper

1 Preheat the grill to hot and line the grill pan with foil. Bring a large pan of water to the boil and cook the potatoes for 15–20 minutes until tender. Drain.

2 Place the haddock fillet skin side down on the grill pan and grill for 5–10 minutes until opaque and cooked through.

3 Meanwhile, heat a large, lidded saucepan and spray with the cooking spray. Stir fry the leeks for a few minutes and then add a couple of tablespoons of water. Cover and leave to cook on a low heat for 5 minutes, or until softened.

4 Add all the other ingredients to the leeks, including the cooked potatoes. Flake in the cooked haddock, removing the skin first and gently fold together. Check the seasoning and heat through, then serve.

3½ **POINTS** values per serving
7½ **POINTS** values per recipe

c **343 calories** per serving

Takes **25 minutes**

✱ not recommended

Baked Plaice with Orange and Tarragon Sauce

Serve with 100 g (3½ oz) baby new potatoes per person and courgettes or green beans, for an extra 1 **POINTS** value per serving.

Serves 4

3 teaspoons half fat butter
560 g (1 lb 3¾ oz) plaice or 8 small fillets
grated zest and juice of a lemon
2 oranges
150 ml (5 fl oz) medium white wine
1 tablespoon chopped fresh tarragon
1 tablespoon chopped fresh parsley
4 tablespoons very low fat plain fromage frais
salt and freshly ground black pepper
a bunch of watercress, to garnish

1 Preheat the oven to Gas Mark 6/200°C/fan oven 180°C. Lightly butter a shallow flameproof roasting tray and arrange the fillets in the bottom. Dot with the remaining butter.

2 Sprinkle the fillets with the lemon zest, half the lemon juice and seasoning.

3 Using a small sharp knife, cut the bottom off the oranges, sit on a board and cut away strips of the peel and pith. Cut each orange into thin, circular slices. Arrange these over the fillets.

4 Pour the wine around the fish. Bake for 10–15 minutes, depending on the thickness of the fillets. Use a fish slice to transfer the fish to warmed serving plates.

5 Place the roasting tin on the hob, over a high heat, and briskly whisk in the remaining lemon juice and herbs. Remove from the heat and add the fromage frais. Season. Spoon alongside the fish. Serve immediately, garnished with fresh watercress sprigs.

3 **POINTS** values per serving
11 **POINTS** values per recipe

C 198 calories per recipe

Takes **15 minutes** to prepare,
15 minutes to cook

✱ not recommended

Ligurian Pizza

A Ligurian pizza is very similar to the Provençal pissaladière and is traditionally topped with onions, black olives and anchovies. The addition of prawns makes it a special treat.

Serves 4

low fat cooking spray
144 g packet pizza base mix
2 onions, sliced
2 garlic cloves, crushed
2 tablespoons thyme leaves
5 anchovies, rinsed and cut in half lengthways
150 g (5½ oz) peeled prawns
10 pitted black olives in brine, drained and sliced
2 tablespoons basil leaves, to garnish

3½ *POINTS* values per serving
13½ *POINTS* values per recipe

C 195 calories per serving

Takes **30 minutes** to prepare, **15 minutes** to cook

✷ not recommended

1 Preheat the oven to Gas Mark 7/220°C/fan oven 200°C. Spray a non stick baking sheet with the cooking spray. Make up the pizza base according to the packet instructions, shaping it into a rectangle about 30 x 18 cm (12 x 7 inches). Place it on the baking tray and set aside.

2 Spray a frying pan with the cooking spray. When it is hot, add the onions and cook over a medium heat for 8 minutes until softened, adding a splash of water if they start to stick. Add the garlic and cook for another 2 minutes. Stir in the thyme leaves, take off the heat and cool slightly.

3 Spread the onion mixture over the pizza base and top with the anchovies. Sprinkle over the prawns and olives and bake for 15 minutes until golden.

4 When the pizza is ready, garnish it with basil leaves before serving.

Variation You can omit the prawns and add 125 g (4½ oz) light mozzarella, drained and sliced, for 5 *POINTS* values per serving.

Grilled Salmon with Hot Mango Salsa

Salsas are a great way to transform a plain meal. This one needs a really juicy, ripe mango for the best sweet and tangy result.

Serves 4

4 x 100 g (3½ oz) boneless salmon fillets
salt and freshly ground black pepper

For the salsa
300 g (10½ oz) mango
finely grated zest and juice of a lime
1 red chilli, de-seeded and chopped finely
1 small red onion, chopped finely

1 Make the salsa. First prepare the mango by cutting each side of the flat stone to remove the flesh. Remove the skin and chop the flesh into small dice, cutting and chopping the flesh that clings to the stone too.

2 In a small bowl, mix together the mango, lime zest and juice, chilli, red onion and a little salt.

3 Cover and chill until ready to serve.

4 Preheat the grill to medium and line the grill pan with foil. Place the salmon fillets skin side up on the grill pan. Season and grill for 2 minutes before turning over. Grill for further 2 minutes, until opaque and cooked through.

5 Serve the salmon with the salsa on the side.

3½ *POINTS* values per serving
14½ *POINTS* values per recipe

234 calories per serving

Takes **20 minutes**

✱ not recommended

Seafood Pasta Shells

Serves 4

300 g (10½ oz) large pasta shells
low fat cooking spray
4 spring onions, chopped finely
400 g (14 oz) seafood selection,
  thawed and drained
2 teaspoons lemon juice
200 g (7 oz) low fat soft cheese
100 ml (3½ fl oz) skimmed milk

1 tablespoon chopped fresh thyme
  or parsley
50 g (1¾ oz) petits pois, fresh or
  frozen
salt and freshly ground black pepper
2 teaspoons thyme sprigs or
  parsley, to garnish

1 Bring a pan of water to the boil and cook the pasta for
  10–12 minutes or according to the instructions on the packet.

2 Meanwhile, spray a large saucepan with the cooking spray. Add the
  spring onions and cook gently, stirring, until softened but not
  browned. Stir in the seafood and lemon juice and cook over a low
  heat for 2–3 minutes. Add the soft cheese, stirring until melted, then
  stir in the milk, herbs, petit pois and seasoning. Heat gently, stirring
  often, for 2 more minutes.

3 Drain the pasta and add it to the seafood mixture, stirring gently to
  mix. Share between four warmed plates and serve at once, garnished
  with the thyme or parsley sprigs.

6½ **POINTS** values per serving
25½ **POINTS** values per recipe

c **402 calories** per serving

Takes **20 minutes**

* not recommended

Simply Vegetables

You don't have to be vegetarian to enjoy vegetables, and this chapter provides plenty of ideas for those looking for a meal without meat. From quick and easy Vegetable Noodles with Ginger and Soy or Mediterranean Pasta Salad, to Spicy Vegetable Tagine and Moroccan Vegetable Stew, there is something here to please everyone.

Why not have a day without meat once in a while and boost your intake of vegetables?

Sicilian Stuffed Peppers

Delicious served with 150 g (5½ oz) cooked rice and a crunchy zero **POINTS** value salad, for an extra 3 **POINTS** values.

Serves 4

4 medium red or yellow peppers, halved lengthways and de-seeded

For the filling

a small bunch of parsley, chopped finely

a small bunch of fresh oregano, chopped finely

2 tablespoons capers, washed, drained, patted dry on kitchen paper then chopped

1 garlic clove, crushed

200 g (7 oz) fresh breadcrumbs

4 ripe tomatoes, skinned, de-seeded and diced finely

2 tablespoons currants

20 stoned black olives in brine, drained and chopped

50 g (1¾ oz) pine kernels, toasted until golden

zest and juice of a lemon

salt and freshly ground black pepper

3½ **POINTS** values per serving
14½ **POINTS** values per recipe

370 calories per serving

Takes **15 minutes** to prepare, **20 minutes** to cook

v

* not recommended

1 Preheat the oven to Gas Mark 6/200°C/fan oven 180°C. Place the peppers cut side up on a baking tray.

2 Mix all the filling ingredients together in a bowl and use to fill the pepper halves. Bake for 20 minutes until tender and golden on top then serve.

Variation Large tomatoes or courgettes can be stuffed with the same mixture, for the same **POINTS** values.

For a non-vegetarian option, add 6 anchovy fillets, drained and chopped finely, for an additional ½ **POINTS** value per serving.

Spicy Bean and Vegetable Supper

Healthy, nutritious, quick and tasty. What more could you ask for when you want good food fast?

Serves 4

low fat cooking spray
1 large red or yellow pepper, de-seeded
   and sliced
125 g (4½ oz) fine green beans, trimmed
   and sliced
1 red (or white) onion, sliced
4 tomatoes, chopped
2 x 420 g cans mixed beans in mild chilli
   sauce
225 g (8 oz) spinach leaves, thoroughly washed
a few drops of Tabasco pepper sauce
salt and freshly ground black pepper
chopped red onion and parsley, to garnish
100 g (3½ oz) tortilla chips, to serve

1 Spray a non stick wok or large frying pan with the cooking spray and heat until hot. Fry the pepper, green beans and onion until softened, about 5 minutes.

2 Add the tomatoes and canned beans. Heat until simmering, then reduce the heat and cook gently for 3–4 minutes.

3 Add the spinach and cook for 3 more minutes, stirring occasionally, until the leaves have wilted down. Check the seasoning, adding Tabasco sauce according to taste.

4 Ladle the mixture onto warmed serving plates and sprinkle with chopped red onion and parsley. Serve with tortilla chips.

4½ **POINTS** values per serving
19 **POINTS** values per recipe

C   **368 calories** per serving

Takes **25 minutes**

V

*   not recommended

Tip If you can't find mixed beans in a chilli or spicy sauce, use ordinary mixed pulses and add extra Tabasco sauce to the recipe, according to taste.

Spinach and Feta Bake

Based on an old Jewish recipe, this is a layered bake with typically Sicilian sweet and sour flavours. Serve with a zero **POINTS** value green salad dressed with lemon.

Serves 4

750 g (1 lb 10 oz) spinach, washed and tough
   stems removed, large leaves shredded
low fat cooking spray
2 garlic cloves, crushed
2 tablespoons capers, rinsed and squeezed to
   remove excess vinegar
3 eggs
1 tablespoon raisins, chopped finely
50 g (1¾ oz) pine nut kernels, toasted
   until golden
450 g (1 lb) carrots, grated
a small bunch of parsley, chopped finely
50 g (1¾ oz) ground almonds
50 g (1¾ oz) Feta cheese
salt and freshly ground black pepper

1 Preheat the oven to Gas Mark 4/180°C/fan oven 160°C

2 Put the wet spinach leaves in a lidded pan, cover and place over a low heat until the spinach has wilted – this should only take a few minutes. Drain and push down into a colander with the back of a large spoon to squeeze out as much of the water as possible. Place in a bowl.

3 Spray a non stick frying pan with the cooking spray and fry the garlic for 1 minute. Add the garlic to the spinach with the capers, and mix together.

4 Lightly beat two of the eggs and add to the spinach mixture, together with the seasoning, raisins and pine nut kernels. Tip into a baking dish and flatten with the back of a large spoon.

5 In a bowl, mix together the carrots with the remaining egg, lightly beaten, parsley and almonds then tip on top of the spinach mixture. Spread out with your fingers then pat down to flatten and compact it.

6 Crumble over the Feta cheese and bake for 35–45 minutes. Serve.

5 **POINTS** values per serving
19½ **POINTS** values per recipe

c 348 **calories** per serving

Takes **30 minutes** to prepare,
45 minutes to cook

v

* not recommended

Sweet Potato Saag Aloo

Try this version of saag aloo for a tasty and unusual change.

Serves 4

700 g (1 lb 9 oz) sweet potatoes, peeled
and cubed
low fat cooking spray
3 cloves
2 teaspoons each mustard seeds and cumin
seeds
1–2 long red chillies, de-seeded and cut into
long strips
3 large garlic cloves, chopped
5 cm (2 inch) fresh root ginger, peeled and
chopped finely
400 g (14 oz) spinach, leaves shredded
4 tablespoons low fat natural yogurt
salt and freshly ground black pepper

2½ *POINTS* values per serving
10 *POINTS* values per recipe

C   **201 calories** per serving

Takes **25 minutes**

V

*   recommended

1 Bring a pan of water to the boil, add the sweet potatoes and cook for 10–12 minutes until tender. Drain well.

2 Spray a large, heavy based, non stick frying pan with the cooking spray and fry the cloves, mustard seeds and cumin seeds until they start to pop and smell aromatic.

3 Add the chillies, garlic, ginger and spinach and stir fry for 2 minutes until the spinach has wilted. Stir in the sweet potato, 3 tablespoons of water and the yogurt. Season well and cook for 1–2 minutes, stirring frequently until combined. Serve immediately.

Moroccan Vegetable Stew

Turn vegetables into this colourful, flavoursome stew that the whole family will love.

Serves 2

1 red pepper
1 green pepper
low fat cooking spray
1 onion, sliced
1 garlic clove, crushed
1 fresh red chilli, de-seeded and chopped
1 teaspoon ground cumin
1 small aubergine, sliced thinly
225 g (8 oz) plum tomatoes, skinned,
    de-seeded and chopped
150 ml (5 fl oz) vegetable stock or tomato
    juice
salt and freshly ground black pepper
2 tablespoons chopped fresh coriander, to garnish

---

0 POINTS value per serving
0 POINTS values per recipe

C   **100 calories** per serving

Takes **30 minutes** to cook + **15 minutes** standing

V

✱   recommended

1   Preheat the grill to hot. Place the peppers under the grill, turning frequently, until the skin is charred and blistered. Put in a plastic bag and leave to cool.

2   Spray a lidded saucepan with the cooking spray and heat until hot. Add the onion, garlic and chilli and cook gently for 5 minutes, until softened but not coloured, adding a splash of water if they start to stick. Add the cumin and cook for 1 minute more.

3   Halve the aubergine slices and add to the pan, then add the tomatoes and stock or tomato juice. Season with black pepper. Simmer for 20 minutes, partly covered, stirring occasionally.

4   Meanwhile, peel the peppers, discarding the skins, cores and seeds. Cut the flesh into thin strips.

5   Five minutes before the end of cooking, stir the pepper strips into the aubergine mixture. Season to taste. Serve, garnished with chopped coriander.

Gnocchi with Quick Tomato Sauce

Fast, easy and tasty, this is the perfect supper for the end of a busy day.

Serves 2

350 g (12 oz) packet fresh, chilled gnocchi
1 tablespoon grated Parmesan cheese
torn basil leaves, to garnish

For the tomato sauce

1 small onion, chopped finely
½ tablespoon tomato purée
400 g can chopped tomatoes with chilli
150 ml (5 fl oz) vegetable stock
½ teaspoon sugar
salt and freshly ground black pepper

1 Place all the ingredients for the tomato sauce in a saucepan. Bring to the boil and simmer vigorously, uncovered, for about 20 minutes until the liquid has been reduced to a thick sauce. Season to taste.

2 Meanwhile, cook the gnocchi according to the packet instructions. Drain and set aside. Preheat the grill to high.

3 Spoon a little sauce in the base of two shallow, flameproof bowls. Add the gnocchi, then pour the remaining sauce over. Sprinkle with the cheese. Grill for 2 minutes until the cheese turns golden brown.

4 Scatter the basil leaves over and serve immediately.

4 POINTS values per serving
8 POINTS values per recipe

C **350 calories** per serving

Takes **30 minutes**

V

✳ recommended (sauce only)

Vegetable Noodles with Ginger and Soy

Bursting with freshness, this quick stir fry is filling and full of flavour.

Serves 4

250 g (9 oz) medium egg noodles
low fat cooking spray
2.5 cm (1 inch) fresh root ginger,
   peeled and grated
1 garlic clove, crushed
175 g (6 oz) carrots, cut into thin
   sticks
2 celery stalks, trimmed and sliced
150 g (5½ oz) mushrooms, sliced

175 g (6 oz) courgettes, trimmed
   and cut into sticks
100 g (3½ oz) mange tout, trimmed
100 g (3½ oz) baby corn, trimmed
   and halved
6 spring onions, trimmed and sliced
3 tablespoons soy sauce
1 tablespoon medium sherry

1 Place the noodles in a bowl and pour boiling water over. Leave to stand for 10 minutes.

2 Meanwhile spray a large frying pan or wok with the cooking spray and stir fry the ginger, garlic, carrots, celery, mushrooms, courgettes, mange tout and baby corn for 5 minutes.

3 Drain the noodles thoroughly and toss into the vegetables with the spring onions, soy sauce and sherry. Cook for 2 to 3 minutes more.

3 POINTS values per serving
12½ POINTS values per recipe

C **269 calories** per serving

Takes **25 minutes**

V

* recommended

Tip When you buy a piece of root ginger, keep what you don't use in the freezer so you can just grate a little as and when you need it.

Mushroom Toad in the Hole with Onion Gravy

A firm family favourite, with added vegetables to increase your daily intake.

Serves 4

1 tablespoon olive oil
200 g (7 oz) open cap mushrooms
1 onion, cut into wedges
8 Quorn sausages
125 g (4½ oz) wholemeal plain flour
a pinch of salt
1 egg
300 ml (10 fl oz) skimmed milk
salt and freshly ground black pepper

For the onion gravy
low fat cooking spray
1 onion, sliced thinly
500 ml (18 fl oz) vegetable stock
2 tablespoons wholemeal plain flour
1 teaspoon Marmite

5½ **POINTS** values per serving
22 **POINTS** values per recipe

351 **calories** per serving

Takes **20 minutes** to prepare,
35 minutes to cook

v

* not recommended

1 Preheat the oven to Gas Mark 7/220°C/fan oven 200°C. Pour the olive oil into a non stick roasting tin measuring 19 x 23 cm (7½ x 9 inches) and toss the mushrooms, onion wedges and sausages in the oil to coat. Cook for 10 minutes until golden.

2 Meanwhile, sift the flour into a mixing bowl with a pinch of salt, tipping in any bran from the sieve. Make a well in the centre and break in the egg. Gradually whisk in the milk to give a smooth batter. Season. Pour the batter over the sausages and vegetables and return to the oven to cook for 20–25 minutes, until the batter is risen, crisp and golden.

3 To make the gravy, spray a medium, lidded saucepan with the cooking spray and fry the sliced onion for 5 minutes until well browned. If necessary, add a little water to prevent the onion from sticking. Add 3 tablespoons of the stock, cover the pan and cook gently for 10 minutes until the onion is completely soft.

4 Stir in the flour, followed by the rest of the stock and the Marmite. Bring to the boil and simmer, uncovered for 5 minutes. Season with black pepper to taste and serve with the toad in the hole.

Variation For a non-vegetarian version, replace the vegetarian sausages with low fat pork sausages, for the same **POINTS** values per serving.

Pea and Herb Risotto

This delicious summery dish can also be made with fresh peas when in season.

Serves 4

850 ml (1½ pints) vegetable stock
250 g (9 oz) frozen petit pois
4 tablespoons each chopped fresh mint
   and parsley
low fat cooking spray
1 large onion, chopped finely
1 leek, chopped finely
2 large garlic cloves, chopped finely
240 g (8½ oz) risotto rice
150 ml (5 fl oz) dry white wine
salt and freshly ground black pepper
15 g (½ oz) Parmesan cheese, grated
   coarsely, to serve

4½ *POINTS* values per serving
18½ *POINTS* values per recipe

C   **321 calories** per serving

Takes **40 minutes**

V

✱   recommended

1 Heat the stock in a saucepan and add half of the petit pois. When cooked, scoop the petit pois out using a slotted spoon and transfer to a food processor, or use a hand blender, with a small ladleful of stock and the herbs. Process until puréed and set aside.

2 Spray a large, heavy based, lidded saucepan with the cooking spray and fry the onion and leek, half covered, for 9 minutes or until softened – occasionally adding a little water to the pan if necessary. Add the garlic and fry for another minute.

3 Add the rice and stir until coated in the onion mixture. Pour in the wine and bring to the boil. Reduce the heat and simmer until the wine is absorbed and the smell of alcohol disappears.

4 Add a ladleful of stock and simmer, stirring, until it is absorbed. Continue to add the stock a ladleful at a time until the liquid is almost fully absorbed and the rice is tender and creamy in texture; this will take 20–25 minutes.

5 Stir in the pea purée and the rest of the peas and heat through.

6 Season and serve sprinkled with Parmesan.

Ratatouille Pasta Bake

You can make the ratatouille ahead of time so that it is quick to assemble, then bake it when you come in from work.

Serves 4

low fat cooking spray
2 onions, sliced
1 aubergine, cut into 2 cm (¾ in) chunks
2 small courgettes, cut into 1 cm (½ in) dice
1 red and 1 green pepper, de-seeded and
    sliced
2 garlic cloves, crushed
2 x 400 g cans chopped tomatoes
150 ml (5 fl oz) vegetable stock
125 ml (4 fl oz) red wine
2 sprigs of fresh rosemary
2 bay leaves
250 g (9 oz) strozzapreti or fusilli pasta
salt and freshly ground black pepper

To serve
2 tablespoons grated Parmesan cheese
crisp green salad leaves

4 POINTS values per serving
17 POINTS values per recipe

C **347 calories** per serving

Takes **15 minutes** to prepare,
1 hour to cook

V

＊ not recommended

1 Spray a large lidded pan with the cooking spray and heat until sizzling. Add the onions and cook for 5 minutes until softened.

2 Spray the aubergine, courgettes and peppers with the cooking spray and add to the pan. Cook, stirring, over a medium heat for 5 minutes then add the garlic, tomatoes, stock, wine and herbs.

3 Bring to the boil, reduce the heat, cover and simmer for 30 minutes. The mixture should be very juicy. Season.

4 Preheat the oven to Gas Mark 5/190°C/fan oven 170°C. Spray a large baking dish with the cooking spray. Mix the pasta into the ratatouille ensuring it is evenly coated, then spoon it into the baking dish. Cover with foil and bake for 30 minutes until the pasta is just cooked.

5 Remove the bay leaves, sprinkle the cheese over the top and serve with the salad leaves.

Tips Ratatouille is best left in the fridge overnight to allow the flavours to develop.

You can use the ratatouille tossed into boiled pasta if you prefer. Just reheat it in a saucepan over a medium heat for 2–3 minutes, until piping hot.

Spicy Vegetable Tagine

If you wish, add 150 g (5½ oz) cooked brown rice per person, for an extra 3 **POINTS** values per serving.

Serves 4

low fat cooking spray
2 onions, chopped
3 garlic cloves, chopped finely
600 g (1 lb 5 oz) butternut squash, peeled, de-seeded and cut into 1 cm (½ inch) dice
1 tablespoon each ground cumin and ground coriander
1 teaspoon each cinnamon, hot chilli powder and turmeric
2 x 400 g cans chopped tomatoes
2 teaspoons tomato purée
2 courgettes, thickly sliced
400 g can chick peas, drained and rinsed
400 g can apricots in juice, drained
salt and freshly ground black pepper
2 tablespoons fresh coriander, to garnish

1½ **POINTS** values per serving
6 **POINTS** values per recipe

C **250 calories** per serving

Takes **30 minutes** to prepare,
15 minutes to cook

V

* recommended

1 Spray a large, heavy based, lidded saucepan with the cooking spray and fry the onions for 8–10 minutes or until softened, adding a little water if necessary to prevent from sticking.

2 Spray with more cooking spray, add the garlic and fry for 1 minute, again adding more water if required. Add the squash to the pan with the spices and cook for another minute.

3 Add the tomatoes, tomato purée and 150 ml (5 fl oz) water. Bring to the boil then reduce the heat and simmer, covered, for 10 minutes.

4 Stir in the courgettes and chick peas. Slice the apricots and add to the pan. Season and cook, partially covered, for 10–15 minutes until the vegetables are tender. Add a little extra water if the tagine appears dry.

5 Serve sprinkled with the fresh coriander.

One Pot Veggie Curry

This delicious curry is crammed full of multi coloured vegetables to give a variety of nutrients. Any leftover curry is wonderful spooned over a crisp-skinned 225 g (8 oz) jacket potato per person, for a *POINTS* value of 2½ per serving.

Serves 4

low fat cooking spray
1 onion, chopped roughly
1 red and 1 yellow pepper, de-seeded and
    chopped roughly
2 teaspoons grated fresh root ginger
2 garlic cloves, crushed
1 tablespoon medium curry powder
500 g (1 lb 2 oz) potatoes, peeled and diced
225 g (8 oz) cauliflower florets
850 ml (1½ pints) vegetable stock
110 g (4 oz) red lentils, rinsed
150 g (5½ oz) green beans, trimmed and cut
    into thirds
salt and freshly ground black pepper
chopped fresh coriander, to serve

1 Spray a large, lidded saucepan or flameproof casserole dish with the cooking spray and brown the onion for 2 minutes. Tip the peppers into the pan and stir fry for a further 2 minutes. Stir in the ginger, garlic and curry powder and cook for 30 seconds.

2 Add the potatoes and cauliflower to the pan and stir to coat in the spice mixture, then pour in the vegetable stock and lentils. Mix together well and season lightly. Bring the mixture to a simmer, cover the pan and cook for 10 minutes.

3 Stir the green beans into the curry, replace the lid and cook gently for a further 10 minutes or until the lentils have broken down to thicken the sauce and the vegetables are tender. Scatter with coriander before serving.

2½ *POINTS* values per serving
10½ *POINTS* values per recipe

253 calories per serving

Takes **15 minutes** to prepare,
20 minutes to cook

V

* not recommended

Mediterranean Pasta Salad

This is an ideal recipe for a griddle pan. Otherwise grill the vegetables in batches under the grill or bake them in a hot oven.

Serves 4

240 g (8½ oz) penne or other pasta
   shapes
2 red onions, cut into thin wedges
4 courgettes, cut lengthways into
   long strips
2 red peppers, de-seeded and
   sliced

2 aubergines, sliced lengthways
   into long thin pieces
low fat cooking spray
100 g (3½ oz) Feta cheese
a bunch of mint, chopped
2 garlic cloves, crushed
2 tablespoons balsamic vinegar
salt and freshly ground black pepper

1 Bring a pan of water to the boil, add the pasta and cook according to the packet instructions. Drain. Preheat the grill to hot.

2 Lay the vegetables in one layer on a grill pan and season. Spray with the cooking spray and grill for 4–5 minutes until the vegetables are golden and beginning to crisp. You may have to grill them in several batches depending on the size of your grill pan. Place them in a large bowl.

3 Add the cooked pasta, Feta cheese, mint, garlic and balsamic vinegar to the bowl, check the seasoning, toss together and serve.

5 **POINTS** values per serving
20 **POINTS** values per recipe

C 355 calories per serving

Takes 25 minutes

V

* not recommended

Porcini with Red and Yellow Pepper Pasta

Dried porcini have an intense mushroom flavour, which is particularly good in this colourful mixture.

Serves 2

25 g packet porcini mushrooms
125 g (4½ oz) farfalle or pasta bows
low fat cooking spray
1 red pepper, de-seeded and sliced
1 yellow pepper, de-seeded and sliced
2 heads pak choi, leaves separated
8 sage leaves
1 tablespoon mushroom ketchup or soy sauce

3 *POINTS* values per serving
6 *POINTS* values per recipe

C 298 calories per serving

Takes **25 minutes** + **20 minutes** soaking

V

✱ not recommended

1 Put the porcini mushrooms in a bowl and cover with boiling water. Leave to soak for 20 minutes then drain, reserving 1 tablespoon of the liquid.

2 Bring a large pan of water to the boil, add the pasta and cook for 10–12 minutes or according to packet instructions. Drain and rinse with boiling water.

3 Meanwhile, spray a large frying pan or wok with cooking apray, add the peppers and porcini and stir fry for 3 minutes. Add the pak choi and sage and continue cooking for 3–4 minutes until the peppers have softened. You may need to add a splash of water if they start to stick.

4 Add the pasta, mushroom ketchup or soy sauce and the reserved porcini soaking liquid and heat for 1–2 minutes until everything is hot. Serve immediately.

Tip Porcini are dried mushrooms. They are readily available in supermarkets, usually in the section with pasta sauces.

Variation If you want to make this a super quick dish, use 150 g (5½ oz) of fresh mushrooms and cut out the soaking time, for the same *POINTS* values per serving.

Desserts in Minutes

Desserts don't have to be fattening and full of sugar. Try these delicious recipes, all of which can be made quickly and easily. You'll love Chocolate Orange Treat and Banana and Chocolate Fool, and there are plenty of yummy ideas with fruit, including Lemon and Berry Creamy Pots and Quick Baked Apples with Plums and Sultanas. Enjoy.

Delicious desserts don't have to be complicated

Chocolate Orange Treat

This luscious layered dessert is perfect for a special occasion. It only takes a few minutes to put together and it tastes divine.

Serves 4

4 tablespoons whipping cream
125 g pot low fat orange yogurt
2 oranges, scrubbed
8 ginger thins
40 g (1½ oz) dark chocolate
mint or lemon balm leaves, to decorate

4½ *POINTS* values per serving
18½ *POINTS* values per recipe

C **197 calories** per serving

Takes **15 minutes**

V

✻ not recommended

1 In a chilled bowl, whip the cream until it holds its shape. Fold in the yogurt. Chill for a few minutes.

2 Meanwhile, use a zester to remove the zest from 1 orange. Reserve for decoration. Finely grate the zest from the other orange and fold through the cream mixture.

3 Using a sharp serrated knife, remove all the peel and pith from the oranges, then cut them into segments, removing all the membrane.

4 On separate serving plates, layer the biscuits with the cream mixture and orange segments.

5 Melt the chocolate in a bowl placed over a saucepan of gently simmering water, then use to drizzle over the desserts. Decorate with the reserved orange zest and mint or lemon balm leaves.

Tip Serve these desserts shortly after you've made them, or else the biscuits will go soggy.

Papaya Yogurt Brûlée

A simply delicious taste and texture combination that can be put together in minutes.

Serves 4

1 large ripe papaya, peeled and chopped into large pieces
juice of ½ a lime
500 g (1 lb 2 oz) 0% fat Greek yogurt
4 teaspoons light muscovado sugar

1 Preheat the grill to high. Place the papaya in the base of an ovenproof dish, or use four individual ramekin dishes, and squeeze over the lime juice.

2 Top with the yogurt and then sprinkle with the brown sugar. Place under the grill for a few minutes, watching carefully, until the sugar has caramelised. Serve immediately.

2 **POINTS** values per serving
7½ **POINTS** values per recipe

C **115 calories** per serving

Takes **10 minutes**

V

* not recommended

Amaretti Peaches

Amaretti biscuits with peaches are a real Italian treat. If you can spare the **POINTS** values, top the peaches with a tablespoon of low fat natural yogurt, for an additional ½ **POINTS** value per serving.

Serves 2

2 ripe peaches
3 amaretti biscuits
1 egg white
1 tablespoon reduced sugar apricot jam

1 Preheat the oven to Gas Mark 4/180°C/fan oven 160°C.

2 Cut the peaches in half and take out the stones. Lay them cut side up on a baking tray.

3 Crush the amaretti biscuits with your hands. In a clean, grease free bowl, whisk the egg white until it holds stiff peaks.

4 Fold the amaretti biscuits and jam into the egg white then divide this mixture between the four peach halves.

5 Cook in the oven for 8–10 minutes, until the tops are golden.

1½ **POINTS** values per serving
2½ **POINTS** values per recipe

C   **195 calories** per serving

Takes **20 minutes**

V

✳   not recommended

Variation Try using six plums or apricots for this dish in place of the peaches, for the same **POINTS** values per serving.

Strawberry Custards

Make this dessert in advance so it is ready to whip out of the fridge when needed.

Serves 2

300 ml (10 fl oz) skimmed milk
2 eggs, beaten
½ x 11 g sachet gelatine
300 g (10½ oz) strawberries, hulled
1 tablespoon artificial sweetener

2½ **POINTS** values per serving
5 **POINTS** values per recipe

191 calories per serving

Takes 15 minutes + 2 hours chilling

* not recommended

1 Heat the milk in a saucepan to just below boiling point. Remove from the heat, stir in the eggs and then bring back to the boil, stirring continuously until thickened.

2 Dissolve the gelatine according to the packet instructions and stir into the custard. Cover the surface with clingfilm to prevent a skin forming and set aside to cool slightly.

3 Set four strawberries to one side and blend the remaining ones in a liquidiser. Stir the strawberry purée into the custard with the artificial sweetener.

4 Pour into two individual shallow dishes. Chop the reserved strawberries and decorate the top of the custards. Leave to cool completely before chilling for 2 hours to set.

Raspberry Charlotte

Quick and easy and a great way to use up stale bread.

Serves 2

300 g (10½ oz) fresh raspberries
2½ tablespoons artificial sweetener
25 g (1 oz) low fat polyunsaturated margarine
4 slices of day old white bread, crusts removed
1 teaspoon ground cinnamon
low fat cooking spray

1 Put the raspberries in a small saucepan with 1 tablespoon of water and 2 tablespoons of sweetener. Cook over a low heat until the juices run from the fruit.

2 Meanwhile, spread the margarine on the bread. Mix the cinnamon and the remaining sweetener together then sprinkle this over the bread. Cut into triangles.

3 Spray a small baking dish, or two individual ramekin dishes, with the cooking spray. Spoon the raspberries into the dish and arrange the bread on top, cinnamon side up.

4 Just before serving, heat the grill to hot and grill for 5–10 minutes, or until the top is golden brown and crisp and the fruit is bubbling up at the edges.

4½ *POINTS* values per serving
9½ *POINTS* values per recipe

C **265 calories** per serving

Takes **20 minutes**

V

✳ not recommended

Quick Baked Apples with Plums and Sultanas

This easy dessert will satisfy your sweet tooth, without piling up the **POINTS** values. If you wish, rather than microwaving, cook this dessert in the oven at Gas Mark 4/180°C/fan oven 160°C for 40 minutes.

Serves 4

4 cooking apples, peeled and cored
6 plums, stoned and sliced
1 heaped tablespoon sultanas
artificial sweetener, to taste
4 heaped tablespoons reduced-sugar strawberry jam

1 Put the apples in a microwaveable dish. Mix the plums with the sultanas and use this mixture to fill the cavities in the apples.

2 Sprinkle the apples with artificial sweetener, then place a heaped tablespoon of strawberry jam on top of each one.

3 Cook in the microwave on High for 6–8 minutes, or until the apples are tender and the jam has melted.

4 Serve the apples with the hot syrupy mixture spooned over and around them.

2½ **POINTS** values per serving
11 **POINTS** values per recipe

C 130 **calories** per serving

⊙ Takes **15 minutes** to prepare, **8 minutes** to cook

V

✱ not recommended

Variation For a real treat, serve the apples with a small (150 g) pot of low fat custard per person, for an extra 2 **POINTS** values per serving.

White Chocolate Mousses with Strawberries

Dip to the bottom of these rich chocolate pots to find a tangy strawberry sauce.

Serves 4

150 g (5½ oz) strawberries

110 g (4 oz) good quality white chocolate, broken into squares

1 tablespoon skimmed milk

3 egg whites

1 Reserve two strawberries for decoration and purée the rest with a hand blender or in a liquidiser. Divide between four 150 ml (5 fl oz) ramekins.

2 Place the chocolate in a bowl and melt in a microwave or over a pan of simmering water. Add the milk and stir to combine. Cool slightly.

3 In a clean, grease free bowl, whisk the egg whites until they form soft peaks. Add 1 tablespoon of the whisked egg whites to the chocolate and quickly combine. Carefully fold the remaining egg whites into the chocolate mixture.

4 Spoon the chocolate mixture on top of the strawberry purée and chill for at least 2 hours until set.

5 Slice the reserved strawberries and use to decorate before serving.

3½ *POINTS* values per serving
13½ *POINTS* values per recipe

C **165 calories** per serving

Takes **15 minutes** + **2 hours** chilling

V

* not recommended

Variation If you fancy a change, you can make this with 110 g (4 oz) milk chocolate instead of white, for the same *POINTS* values per serving.

Brûléed Kiwi and Grape Cheesecakes

These wonderful individual cheesecakes have a delicious twist – they are finished under the grill to give a crunchy brûlée topping.

Serves 4

4 low fat digestive biscuits, crushed
4 tablespoons medium sweet sherry
3 kiwi fruit, peeled and sliced
100 g (3½ oz) seedless red or green grapes
200 g (7 oz) Quark
150 g (5½ oz) very low fat natural yogurt
½ teaspoon vanilla essence
4 teaspoons light brown demerera sugar

1 Sprinkle half the biscuit crumbs into the base of four heatproof teacups or ramekin dishes. Sprinkle ½ tablespoon of sherry over the top of each.

2 Mix together the kiwi fruit and grapes. Divide half of the mixture between the four dishes.

3 Beat the Quark in a bowl to soften it, then mix in the yogurt and vanilla essence. Spoon half the mixture over the fruit. Repeat all the layers once more.

4 Cover and chill for 10 minutes, or until almost ready to serve.

5 Preheat a grill to hot. Sprinkle 1 heaped teaspoon of demerara sugar over each dessert to cover the surface. Grill until the sugar melts and bubbles. Cool for a few moments, then serve.

3 POINTS values per serving
11½ POINTS values per recipe

C **191 calories** per serving

Takes **20 minutes** +
10 minutes chilling

V

✱ not recommended

Variation If you don't wish to use sherry, use 4 tablespoons of unsweetened white grape juice or orange juice instead, for 2½ **POINTS** values per serving.

Lemon and Berry Creamy Pots

If you're looking for a sweet indulgence, try this version of cheesecake – it's so luscious that you won't even miss the usual biscuit base.

Serves 4

zest and juice of a lemon
12 g sachet gelatine powder
200 g (7 oz) low fat soft cheese
250 g (9 oz) low fat natural yogurt
5 tablespoons artificial sweetener
250 g (9 oz) frozen summer berries mix, defrosted

2½ *POINTS* values per serving
9 *POINTS* values per recipe

C **131 calories** per serving

Takes **15 minutes** + **1 hour** chilling

* not recommended

1 Pour the lemon juice into a small heatproof bowl and sprinkle the gelatine over. Leave to stand for 3 minutes to absorb the liquid and then stand the bowl in a small saucepan of gently simmering water and leave to melt.

2 Meanwhile, mix together the lemon zest, soft cheese, yogurt and 4 tablespoons of sweetener in a mixing bowl until smooth. Pour in the melted gelatine and stir to combine evenly.

3 Divide the mixture between four 200 ml (7 fl oz) glasses, cover with clingfilm and chill in the fridge for 1 hour or until firm.

4 Mix the defrosted berries with the remaining sweetener and spoon on top of the pots just before serving.

Variation For a strawberry version, replace the low fat natural yogurt with low fat strawberry yogurt, and top with 150 g (5½ oz) sliced strawberries in place of the summer berries. The *POINTS* values per serving will remain the same.

Poached Peaches in Vanilla Syrup

A simple recipe that even works wonders for under ripe or tasteless peaches or nectarines.

Serves 4

2 teaspoons artificial sweetener
1 vanilla pod, sliced in half lengthways
4 ripe peaches, sliced in half and stoned

1 Pour 300 ml (10 fl oz) of water into a large saucepan then add the artificial sweetener and vanilla pod. Arrange the peaches cut side down in the pan and heat until boiling.

2 Boil for a few minutes and then turn off the heat. Allow to cool before serving two peach halves per person, with some of the syrup spooned over.

½ *POINTS* value per serving
2 *POINTS* values per recipe

C   **55 calories** per serving

⊘   Takes **10 minutes**

V   **Vg**

✳   not recommended

Peach Melba

Peach Melba was a dish created in honour of the opera singer, Dame Nellie Melba, and is a classic summery combination of peaches and raspberries. Using tinned peaches and frozen raspberries means that you can enjoy this dessert all year round.

Serves 4

200 g (7 oz) fresh or frozen raspberries, defrosted
1 tablespoon artificial sweetener, plus an extra 2 teaspoons
2 x 411 g cans peach halves in juice, drained
175 g (6 oz) low fat soft cheese
few drops almond extract

1 In a liquidiser or with a hand held blender, whizz the raspberries to a purée with 1 tablespoon sweetener. Press through a sieve to remove the seeds.

2 Place the peach halves in a large bowl.

3 Mix the soft cheese with 2 teaspoons sweetener and a couple of drops of almond extract, then spoon the mixture into the bowl with the peach halves.

4 Serve with the raspberry sauce poured over the peaches.

2 *POINTS* values per serving
8 *POINTS* values per recipe

C 122 calories per serving

Takes 10 minutes

V

✳ not recommended

Speedy Sticky Pears

A fantastically fast pudding fix, complete with a creamy accompaniment.

Serves 2

410 g can pear halves in natural juice, drained
1½ teaspoons artificial sweetener
low fat cooking spray

For the cinnamon fromage frais
100 g (3½ oz) low fat plain fromage frais
pinch of ground cinnamon

---

2 POINTS values per serving
3½ POINTS values per recipe

C   **89 calories** per serving

Takes **5 minutes**

V

✳   not recommended

1 Heat a non stick frying pan on a medium to high heat. Drain the pears and dry on a kitchen towel. Sprinkle over half a teaspoon of the sweetener. Lightly coat the frying pan with the cooking spray, add the pears and cook for 2 minutes each side until caramelized.

2 Meanwhile, mix the fromage frais together with the cinnamon and the remaining sweetener. Spoon over the caramelised pears to serve.

Grilled Pineapple in Lemongrass Syrup

A very simple but exotically flavoured dessert. Delicious served with 2 tablespoons of low fat natural yogurt or virtually fat free fromage frais per person, for an extra ½ **POINTS** value per serving.

Serves 6

**1 pineapple, peeled and cut
    into rounds**
**1–2 lemongrass stalks, chopped into short
    lengths and beaten with a rolling pin**
2 tablespoons artificial sweetener

1 Preheat the grill to medium. Grill the pineapple slices for 5 minutes on each side, until golden, then place on serving plates.

2 Meanwhile, in a small saucepan, bring 300 ml (10 fl oz) of water to the boil with the lemongrass and sweetener. Simmer for 5 minutes, or until the water is infused with the lemongrass flavour.

3 Strain the syrup over the pineapple and serve immediately.

½ **POINTS** value per serving
3 **POINTS** values per recipe

C   **30 calories** per serving

Takes **15 minutes**

V   **Vg**

✱   not recommended

Banana and Chocolate Fool

This rich tasting pudding is an excellent way to use up bananas that are past their best.

Serves 4

2 large ripe bananas
juice of a small lemon
2 teaspoons artificial sweetener or to taste (optional)
200 g pot very low fat plain fromage frais
20 g (¾ oz) dark chocolate, grated finely

1 Blend the bananas in a food processor with the lemon juice and sweetener, if using.

2 Transfer the banana mixture to a mixing bowl and fold in the fromage frais.

3 Divide the mixture between four sundae or ramekin dishes. Sprinkle over the grated chocolate and chill in the refrigerator until firm.

2 *POINTS* values per serving
7 *POINTS* values per recipe

C 120 calories per serving

Takes 12 minutes + chilling

V

* not recommended

Index